SUPERHERO SECRETS FOR TEACHERS

BEHAVIOR ANALYSIS IN THE CLASSROOM

Natalie L. Perkel, Ph.D., BCBA
Beverly G. Smith, M.Ed., BCBA, LBA

ISBN 979-8-9858678-0-0 (Paperback)
ISBN 979-8-9858678-1-7 (eBook)

Library of Congress Control Number 2022936075

All examples and events in this book are fictitious. Any similarity to real persons, living or dead, is coincidental and not intended by the authors.

Edited by Sarah Reilley
Cover Design by Pankaj Singh
Interior Design and Formatting by

www.emtippettsbookdesigns.com
Images included in the book are property of Behavior Queens, Inc.

Printed in the United States of America

Published by Behavior Queens, LLC

behaviorqueens@gmail.com
www.facebook.com/behaviorqueens
Instagram @behaviorqueens

Your academic career can prepare you to be an effective teacher.
Your creative abilities will assist you in presenting material...but this book!
This book will help you become a behavior superhero!

For our families:
Thank you for your unending love & support.

To our S6 girls:
Thank you for being such an amazing resource and sounding board on all things BCBA-related.

Contents

Chapter 1:

Getting Started with Applied Behavior Analysis (ABA)

Introduction

Imagine this: You're a third-grade teacher and you've just started a math lesson. You tell your students to complete ten problems quietly. One of your students begins to whine. You continue with the lesson, but his whining is getting louder and louder. The other students grow distracted. You send the student to sit in the hall. The next day, the same situation occurs. And the next. And the next. Why does this keep happening?

Has a similar situation ever happened to you? Have you ever wondered why a specific student acts in a certain way?

The purpose of this book is to introduce Applied Behavior Analysis (ABA) and show how it can be implemented in the classroom. ABA does not offer a "quick fix" and it is a highly involved scientific method of behavior change. Because we don't want to overwhelm you, there is a lot of important information not included in this text. This allows us to focus on the fundamentals and allows you to quickly find the information you need to make positive changes in your classroom.

Getting the Most Out of This Book:

- Don't skip stuff (unless we tell you it's ok), as each section builds upon information presented in previous sections.

- Don't read it all at once! We cover a lot of information and it's ALL important. Be sure you have a good understanding of one topic before moving on.

- Keep in mind we are simply giving an introduction to each topic. There is SO much more information on all the subjects that we discuss.

- If there are sections you are familiar with already, read through them anyway. They may include information you need for future sections, or you may be able to expand on your current knowledge.

- Keep an eye out for Superhero Secrets posted throughout the book—they include reminders, tips, and special considerations around a specific topic.

Ethics

Ethics. We know what you're thinking—that it's your favorite topic! Well, you are in luck; it's ours too!

What is ethics? In short (and it is by no means an easy thing to cut short), it is doing the right thing.

Basically, when working in the behavior realm, we are often working to change other people's behavior. With this comes power and we need to be sure that we are always using that power for good. It's like we are superheroes—we need to make the most responsible decisions or people can get hurt. Throughout the text, we will alert you to situations that may have ethical concerns. We do this so that you see that there are ethical considerations around every corner.

Here are some questions to consider related to ethical classroom behavior management:

1. Who is this behavior change going to help?

Let's say a student engages in a behavior that is "annoying" to you. That is NEVER a reason to target a behavior for change. For example, Zane is rocking back and forth in his chair but staying on task. He is not bothering anyone around him. Even if you don't like this behavior, that's not a good enough reason to change it. On the other hand, if the rocking affected his work and became very distracting to others around him, you may need to make some changes. See the difference?

2. What do I do when I don't know what to do?

Don't ever try to do more than you are trained and able to do. When dealing with aggressive, self-injurious, or dangerous behaviors, ALWAYS ask for help from a qualified Board-Certified Behavior Analyst (BCBA). Don't have a BCBA on staff? Be sure to check out the section on collaboration for suggestions on who to turn to in times of trouble. Trying to wing it and figure things out on your own could not only cause someone to get hurt, it could also prolong or increase the behavior.

3. Can I jump around and skip some of the less exciting parts of this process?

Behavior analysis is a science. We have simplified the process as much as possible to provide an introduction on how to use behavior analysis in the classroom. Is it time-consuming? Yes. Do you have 100 other things you are supposed to be doing? Yes. Please remember, we are here to hold your hand along the way. It is preferred that you follow the entire process but sometimes we know it isn't realistic. Be gentle with yourself. Taking baby steps is still progress and using parts of the process is better than nothing.

What is ABA?

ABA is a scientific method of behavior change used to address behaviors by implementing a variety of interventions. It is research-based and most well-known for its treatment of children with autism spectrum disorders (ASD). It is recommended by the U.S. Surgeon General and the American Psychological Association (APA) for the treatment of ASD and is recommended by the Center for Disease Control (CDC) for the treatment of anxiety and attention deficit hyperactivity disorder (ADHD). The truth is that ABA is beneficial for anyone!

ABA can be used to increase behaviors we want to see more of, such as:
- Communication
- Self-help skills
- Academic skills
- Social skills
- Following rules, laws, and guidelines
- Completion of assignments and tasks
- Behavioral self-management
- Emotional regulation

ABA can also be used to decrease behaviors that interfere with learning or are harmful, such as:
- Task refusal
- Elopement
- Physical aggression
- Self-injury

Teachers often use ABA procedures without realizing it, such as when they incorporate visuals or reward correct responses. The good news is you're probably already ahead of the curve!

Seven Dimensions of ABA

Applied Behavior Analysis has "dimensions" or considerations to keep in mind. As you read this section, you may wonder to yourself, "Why are they telling me about this?" Great question! As behavior analysts, we must base our practice on these seven dimensions. You may just skim over this now, but as you come to understand the science of behavior more and more, you will begin to appreciate the seven dimensions as we do. Stay with us here...

The seven characteristics that describe the science of ABA are: generalization, effective, technological, applied, conceptually systematic, analytic, and behavioral.

1. Generalization:

Behaviors or skills don't ONLY occur in the environment in which they are taught. From the start, effective ABA will plan for the generalization of skills to new settings, people, and contexts. For example, you don't want your student to only raise their hand in YOUR classroom; you want them to do the same in the library and other classrooms, as well as with other teachers.

2. Effective:

It is important that you review your students' progress to make sure that your techniques are working. Data on interventions should be closely monitored and evaluated to determine their effects on the targeted behavior.

3. Technological:

The procedures and practices we use are clearly defined so that others can implement them easily and accurately. Think about how you follow a recipe. You gather the ingredients, and then follow each specific direction in order. If you miss a step, you may wind up with something quite different from what you were expecting. We use very specific definitions when discussing behaviors and procedures so everyone working with the child is on the same page and there is no misunderstanding. This is incredibly important. You want to make sure your paraprofessional, the music teacher, and your substitute are all using the same procedures exactly as you designed them.

4. Applied:

We focus only on socially significant behaviors. What does this mean? Think about all those behaviors that take place in your classroom and are getting in the way of your student's success. Aggression? Yep! Refusing to complete their work? That's one! Blurting out answers? Sure! We don't just select behaviors because they get on our nerves, or the parents want them addressed. We only choose behaviors that are having a negative impact on the child. A student quietly tapping their pencil on the desk would not be considered a socially significant behavior unless it interferes with a classmate's learning.

Superhero Secret:
Be sure to keep cultural considerations in mind when selecting goals. For example, different cultures vary on their beliefs regarding appropriate behavior.

Natalie L. Perkel, Ph.D., BCBA & Beverly G. Smith, M.Ed., BCBA, LBA

5. Conceptually Systematic:

All interventions are based on science. We're not just doing trial and error here—our students are not guinea pigs. Everything we do is evidence-based and proven to be effective.

6. Analytic:

All decisions are data-driven. We use that data to determine if our efforts are effective and if we need to make changes to our interventions. We graph our data to provide an easy visual of the increase or decrease in behavior. At first, this may seem like an unnecessary step. But if you give it a try, you will understand its importance. There are many tools out there that can make this task easier for a busy teacher. You can even enlist your students to track their own progress!

7. Behavior:

All targeted behaviors should be observable and measurable. We can see them and take data on them. If we couldn't, we would have no true way to determine if our methods are effective. We would just be guessing otherwise. Don't focus on immeasurable things like "anxiety" or "exhaustion." But we CAN focus on behaviors such as pacing around the room or sleeping during class.

If you're still with us here, good for you! This may not be the "fun" part of ABA, but it is the basis that our practice is built on. Just like a building, ABA can't exist without a strong foundation.

Myths

Feel like you're on the fence about using ABA in your classroom? Maybe you've heard some not-so-great things about ABA. There is a lot of misinformation out there and we want to clear a few things up:

☒ **Myth:** ABA is a new treatment.

☑ **Truth:** Behaviorism dates back to the early 1900s, ABA originated in the early 1930s, and therapists have been using ABA to teach new skills since the early 1960s.

☒ **Myth:** ABA is dangerous.

☑ **Truth:** When implemented correctly under the supervision of a Board-Certified Behavior Analyst (BCBA), it is absolutely NOT dangerous. ABA has inherited this reputation due to its adverse history. In the 60s and 70s, a method called behavior modification became the focus of an investigation when it was discovered that patients in institutions were victims of severe punishment under the veil of ABA therapy. Fortunately, ABA therapy has significantly evolved and now focuses much more on positive reinforcement to encourage changes in behavior.

☒ **Myth:** ABA only takes place at the table.

☑ **Truth:** One teaching method in ABA, known as Discrete Trial Teaching (DTT), often occurs at a table (though not exclusively). DTT breaks down skills into small, specific tasks. ABA can occur anywhere, including on the playground, at guitar lessons, or at the kitchen sink!

☒ **Myth:** ABA turns children into little robots.

☑ **Truth:** Everyone uses some rote memorization in learning, like how students learn their multiplication tables or sight words. Many behaviors are the results of habits that are formed through practice. ABA breaks complex tasks down into simple steps and uses repetition to create a new habit. Those skills are then combined to develop more complex behaviors and can be generalized to new people, places, and activities.

☒ **Myth:** ABA is delivered the same way for each child.
☑ **Truth:** ABA is the science of individual behavior. The reasons individuals engage in certain behaviors are different, so the interventions chosen must also be different.

☒ **Myth:** ABA is only for children with autism.
☑ **Truth:** ABA can be used with children and adults with or without a diagnosis of autism.

If you've heard any of these myths as well, we encourage you to keep an open mind and do your research. ABA can be a game-changer, and it may be just what you need if you give it a chance.

NOTES:

Natalie L. Perkel, Ph.D., BCBA & Beverly G. Smith, M.Ed., BCBA, LBA

Chapter 2:

Eeny, Meeny, Miny, Moe, Which Behavior Has to Go?

What is Behavior?

When we talk about behavior, we are talking about anything that a person does. This includes things we can see (external behaviors), like talking to a friend or smiling, and things we can't see (internal behaviors), like thinking about lunch or listening to a whisper. Just because the last two examples are things that cannot be seen by other people doesn't mean they are not happening in your world.

Another way to understand what behavior IS comes from understanding what it is NOT. Behavior does not include things that happen to us, such as being kicked by someone. It also does not include states of being, like feeling tired or hungry. For the sake of this book, we will focus on observable, measurable, and mostly external behaviors. These are, after all, what you will see most in your classroom.

Superhero Secret:
An easy way to determine if something qualifies as a "behavior" is to use The Dead Man's Test. Ask yourself if a dead man can do it. If the answer is yes, then it's not a behavior. If the answer is no, it is a behavior! Think about it—painting your nails *is* a behavior but having your nails painted *is not*.

Prioritizing Behaviors

There you are, standing in your classroom, looking out at your class. You have plenty of students who are completing the assignment you've given, but then there is Michael who is throwing paper airplanes across the room, Tara who is sleeping, and Ava who is chewing her nails so low that you think you see blood. You want to figure out a solution for each of these situations, but where do you start?

You're in luck! There are guidelines for how to rank the behaviors you want to focus on. In fact, we follow a pretty specific list of questions to make sure to address behaviors in the most responsible and ethical way.

1. Is the behavior dangerous to the student or anyone else? One hundred percent of the time, these are the first behaviors that we address. Examples may include physical aggression, running away from the current setting (elopement), property destruction, or any harmful or self-injurious behaviors (SIB).

2. How often does the behavior occur? Is it happening all day long? Once or twice a week? Did it just happen that one time? Address behaviors that happen more often FIRST. If the behavior isn't

happening very often, you may want to consider if it even needs to be addressed at all.

3. How long has this been going on? Behaviors that have occurred for longer periods of time will need to be addressed before those that just started. For example, Torri has been crying every day for several hours at a time. Recently, she has also started to sing loudly in the cafeteria at lunch. Because the crying behavior has been going on for a longer period of time, it will take precedence over the newer behavior: singing.

4. If we change this behavior, will the person have more of an opportunity to earn reinforcement? For example, if Liza is in a self-contained classroom and has no language skills, teaching her how to ask for what she wants is far more important than teaching her the different parts of a cell. Asking for what she wants will get her what she wants ALL DAY LONG but learning about mitochondria may or may not ever be useful. We aren't sure about you, but we haven't needed that information yet!

5. Will increasing or decreasing this behavior help the student learn new skills or learn to do things by themselves? Think about this in terms of skills that we learn in order to master more complicated skills. Say you are teaching toilet training. Ben will need to be able to pull his pants up and down in front of the toilet. Before that, he will need to learn how to pull his pants up and down during dressing.

6. If we can successfully change this behavior, will other people respond to the student more appropriately? Here's an example: When anyone sits near Molly, she spits on them. None of her classmates want to sit by her. If Molly were to stop spitting on others, she might have the opportunity to make new friends and participate in activities with others. Teaching Molly to tolerate others without spitting will, in turn, encourage others to want to be around Molly.

7. Will others gain from the student producing a new or different behavior? This is a consideration that we have to think about when looking at some behaviors. Sometimes it is relevant to address a behavior in order for others to be able to work with a student. For example, when giving an oral exam, Raj yells out the answers. This interferes with his classmates taking the test. By teaching Raj to instead raise his hand when questions are asked, his peers will have a more positive learning experience.

8. Do you think you can successfully change the behavior? Ask yourself the following questions:

   • What does the research say? There is no need to reinvent the wheel. Try things that people have done and that we already know works.

   • Have you helped a student with this behavior before?

   • How well will you be able to control the variables around you?

   • Are the resources available to change the behavior? This may include time, manpower, materials, etc.

9. Is it worth it? Does the benefit of increasing or decreasing this behavior outweigh the cost of the time, effort, and resources you will put into it?

Once you review the above guidelines, rank the target behaviors accordingly. Make sure that the behaviors fit somewhere in the list above. If it doesn't, it's probably not a behavior that should be targeted. The behavior may fall into more than one category, and that is ok!

Natalie L. Perkel, Ph.D., BCBA & Beverly G. Smith, M.Ed., BCBA, LBA

Superhero Secret:
Make sure you are targeting behaviors for the *right* reasons. Is it
going to have a social impact on the student? If it is just irritating or
frustrating you, then you probably need to reconsider.

Defining Behaviors

Now that you have an idea of the behaviors you need to focus on and which behaviors need to be addressed first, define your target behavior (the behavior you will be focusing on). To do this, write it out in a way that anyone can understand. Eliminate all fancy language and words that require further explanation (such as thinks, needs, or wants). In ABA, we always focus on things that are observable and measurable. How can you measure how much we want this cake? Or how much you need sleep? You can't!

Define your target behavior in very clear terms so that anyone will be able to look at your definition and know exactly what behavior they are looking for (and which behaviors they are not). To do this, we create an operational definition, a specific description of our behavior of interest that includes both what it looks like and a criterion to measure it.

Example: Reno engages in hitting behavior, which can be defined as any occurrence of using an open or closed hand to make forceful contact with any part of another person's body from a distance of four inches or more. An example of hitting would occur if Reno walked over to a classmate who had his pen and hit him to get it back.

A non-example would include Reno giving a friend a high-five.

This is a very specific and clear example, and two or ten people could look at this and would interpret it in almost exactly (if not exactly) the same way.

Incorrect Example: Isa will pay attention in class during work times with 80% accuracy.

This definition is missing a further description of attention and work time, including examples and non-examples.

Natalie L. Perkel, Ph.D., BCBA & Beverly G. Smith, M.Ed., BCBA, LBA

NOTES:

Chapter 3:

Show Me the Data!

Types of Data Collection Measures

"Behavior Analysts say without data, you are just another person with an opinion."
- W. Edwards Deming

D o you HAVE to collect data?
Yes.
Do you have to do it correctly, or can you just check off boxes?
You have to do it correctly.

Sometimes (often), teachers don't take data and just estimate how often a behavior occurs. The problem with this is that we often don't remember the *actual* number of times something happened (especially when 100 other things are going on in the classroom). It may seem like one behavior happens "all the time," but really it only happens during transitions. Also, our personal experiences can skew the number of times we think a behavior occurs. If you have a headache or didn't sleep well last night, it may *seem* like Joel hit another student seventeen times, but in reality, it was only six times today (and far less than last week). Make sense? Recording data as behaviors occur takes the guesswork out of the equation and ensures you are gathering information accurately.

Superhero Secret:

Be sure you take accurate data before building an intervention. Taking a guess at how often the behavior occurs can cause a delay in the treatment process. Record behavior as it is happening. You may think you remember how often it occurred, but your memory may not be accurate.

There are a variety of data collection methods that tell us different things about behaviors. Now that we know exactly what our target behavior is, we have to somehow measure it. Where do we start?

The following categories for measuring a behavior can be used in the classroom:

Data Collection Type	Description
Frequency, rate, duration	Measures each time it occurs
Time sampling (partial, whole, momentary, PLACHECK)	Measures approximately how often they occur
Permanent product	Measures the outcome

Superhero Secret:
Some data is far better than nothing at all. Even if

Natalie L. Perkel, Ph.D., BCBA & Beverly G. Smith, M.Ed., BCBA, LBA

you are not measuring every single occurrence of a behavior, you still get a sample of how often the behavior occurs.

Frequency

Frequency is the number of times a behavior occurs. If all you want to know is how many times it happened, this is the easiest method to collect data. How many students are in your class? Count them up! How many sight words can the student read? Count them! How many days left in the school year? Count! (Although many teachers know this one off the top of their head).

Student Initials: MM
Behavior: Pushing others

Date:	Observer:	Setting:	# of Times:
2/1/21	CB	Classroom	IIII
2/1/21	CB	Music	0
2/1/21	CB	Lunchroom	I
2/1/21	CB	Classroom	II
2/2/21	LR	Class	3

Frequency Data Sheet for Pushing Behavior

Rate

Rate is collected by looking at the number of times a behavior occurs over a specific period of time and is a more popular method to collect data. You may want to measure how many times Adam hits (the behavior) during an eight-hour school day (time). It would look like this: 8x/day or one time per hour. You can use any time component you need for this including minute, hour, class, session, week, year, etc.

Date	Tally of Ind. Requests	Total Ind. Requests	Duration of Observation	Rate
12/2/2020	lllll lllll lllll lllll lllll lllll lllll lllll lll	43	2 hours	21.5/ hour
12/3/2020	lllll lllll lllll llll	19	1 hour	19/ hour
12/4/2020	lllll lllll lllll lllll lllll l	26	2.5 hours	10.4/ hour
12/5/2020	lllll lllll lllll lllll lllll lllll lllll	34	3 hours	11.3/ hour

Rate Data Sheet for Independent Requests

Duration

Duration data is collected when you are interested in how long a behavior occurs. You can measure this with the clock on the wall or the timer on your phone. Start to measure when the behavior starts and stop when the behavior ends. Use duration to measure things like how long it takes for a student to complete a writing assignment, how long they interact with a peer, or how long a student is out of his seat during class.

Student Initials: A.B. **Date:** 10/15/20
Observer: Ms. Thomas **Time:** 1:00 pm

Toy	Time	Total
Mr. Potato Head	1:00- 1:06	6 minutes
Lego table	1:07- 1:09	2m
Trains	1:09- 1:19	10 min

Duration Data Sheet for Toy Play

Natalie L. Perkel, Ph.D., BCBA & Beverly G. Smith, M.Ed., BCBA, LBA

Time Sampling

Time sampling is another great way to measure behavior and is sometimes easier to use in the classroom. This is going to be your next best friend. Although it is not as accurate as other methods, it still provides a snapshot of how often the behavior occurs. YES, it's still better than guessing. We know you don't have time to take data all day long, but we are willing to bet you can carve out five-to-ten minutes to look out for a specific behavior.

There are three types of time sampling: partial interval, whole interval, and momentary time sampling. For all three of these, you break up the total time you observe into smaller pieces. For example, if you observe for ten minutes, you may choose to break this up into ten one-minute intervals.

Interval	1	2	3	4	5	6	7	8	9	10
Behavior (+/-)										

Time Sampling Example

Partial Interval Recording

When measuring for partial interval recording, you look to see if the behavior happened at all during each interval. As soon as you see it happen, you mark it and don't need to mark it again until the next interval. This is a good method that is used for behaviors that you want to *decrease*. Here are a few sample situations in which you could use partial interval:

- *Bryan laughs loudly and it's disrupting for the other students during circle time.*
- *Lena repeatedly looks at her classmate's answers during the spelling test.*

Whole Interval Recording

When looking at whole interval recording, you watch to see if the behavior happens during the ENTIRE interval. If it happens for the first thirty seconds and then stops, you do <u>not</u> mark that interval. This is used for behaviors that you want to *increase*. Below are some examples of times in which you would use whole interval recording:

- *Renee has difficulty remaining quiet during silent reading time.*
- *Lin struggles to attend to an instructional lesson.*

Momentary Time Sampling

Momentary time sampling is the easiest to use but gives you the least accurate information on how often a behavior occurs. You look to see if the student is engaging in the behavior ONLY when the timer goes off (no other time). If they are not, you don't mark the data sheet. If they are engaging in the behavior for the first fifty seconds and then stops right before the timer beeps, you will NOT mark it. Why would you use this? Because sometimes there is limited time to take data, and this will provide a snapshot.

Group Data Collection Procedures

Are you wondering when you're going to have the time to fit in all of this data collection? We have a solution for you! There are two types of data collection measures that are specifically used for groups of students: PLACHECK and permanent product.

Planned Activity Check

Planned Activity Check (PLACHECK) is a type of momentary time sampling that applies to a group. You observe your class and take frequency data on everyone in the group. Let's say your class is working in teams. You glance up at a specific time, count how many people are actively participating in their team project, and mark that on your data sheet. Or maybe you set a timer to go off every 10 minutes during math and quickly take data on who is talking instead of working.

PLACHECK Data Sheet	
Date: March 27	
Time: 11:00 am	
Activity: Choral Responding- Reading Comprehension	
Student Name:	**Behavior:**
J.S.	(On Task) Off task
T.A.	(On Task) Off task
M.A.	On Task (Off task)
A.B.	(On Task) Off task
R.R.	On Task (Off task)
Total Students: 5	**% On Task:** 60%

PLACHECK Data Sheet for Choral Responding Behaviors

Permanent Product

Permanent product is another measurement method that is easy to use with a group of students (yay!). The completed task is proof that the behavior occurred. Examples of permanent products include cleared desks, washed hands, or submitted homework assignments. The example below is a completed worksheet that serves as a permanent product.

Name: Kendall
Date: April 7, 2021

1.	4 x 1 = 4	6.	4 x 7 = 28
2.	4 x 3 = 12	7.	4 x 5 = 20
3.	4 x 9 = 36	8.	4 x 8 = 32
4.	4 x 6 = 24	9.	4 x 4 = 16
5.	4 x 2 = 8	10.	4 x 0 = 0

Example of Permanent Product

Data Collection Guide

Do you only want to know how often it happens? → Frequency

Do you want to know how often it happens in a set amount of time? → Rate

Do you want to know how long the behavior lasts? → Duration

Is this a behavior you want to increase? → Whole interval recording

Is this a behavior you want to decrease? → Partial interval recording

Do you only have a small amount of time to collect data? → Momentary time sampling

Are you looking at the behavior of a group? → PLACHECK

Are you looking at the result of a behavior? → Permanent Product

---

Superhero Secret:
Try to be as sneaky as possible when taking data. We want to avoid affecting the behavior because the student knows you are watching!

Data Collection Methods

Now that you know your target behavior and which type of data you are collecting, you want to pinpoint exactly what happens before and after the target behavior.

You do this by using the ABC model. It breaks down behaviors and looks at what occurs before the behavior (the antecedent) and what occurs after the behavior (the consequence).

(A)ntecedent → (B)ehavior → (C)onsequence

Antecedent	Behavior	Consequence
A child sees a candy bar in the checkout lane at the grocery store.	Whining, flopping on the floor, crying, screaming.	You buy the candy bar.
You tell your teenager to get ready for bed.	They ask you to scratch their back.	You scratch their back for ten minutes.
A guy is sitting next to a girl in class. She isn't paying attention to him.	The guy tells a joke.	The girl laughs.
You ask your child to unload the dishwasher.	They unload the dishwasher.	You tell them they can go play a video game.

Let's analyze this using a real-world example:

You're a third-grade teacher and you've just started a math lesson. You tell your students to complete ten problems quietly. One of your students begins to whine. You continue with the lesson, but his whining is getting louder and louder, distracting the other students. You send the student to sit in the hall. The next day, the same situation occurs.

The behavior you focus on is the student's loud whining. The antecedent (what happens before the behavior) in this scenario is you asking the student to complete the math worksheet. The consequence (what happens after the behavior) is the student being sent to sit in the hall.

Antecedent	Behavior	Consequence
You ask the student to do a worksheet.	Whining.	The student is sent to the hall.

Once you have a good grasp of the different behaviors the student engages in, you can create your own data sheet that is more like a checklist of common antecedents, behaviors, and consequences. For this type of data collection, you will check the boxes with the behaviors that have occurred.

Date/Time	Antecedent (What happened RIGHT before)	Behavior (√ all observed)	Consequence (what happened RIGHT after behavior)
Date: Time: About How long it lasted:	❑ Not doing anything ❑ Interacting with others ❑ Told to do something (complete a task, etc) ❑ Something was taken away ❑ Asked to leave a location ❑	❑ picking (lips, fingers, toes) ❑ Self Injury – hitting head or ___ ❑ Hitting others ❑ Kicking others ❑ Screaming ❑ crying - Tears? Yes/No ❑	❑ Ignored ❑ Lost privileges (toy/item he had) ❑ Talked to him ("you can't do that" or "let's talk about what happened") ❑ Redirected him ("let's go outside" or "go get your book") ❑ Got what he wanted ❑
Date: Time: About How long it lasted:	❑ Not doing anything ❑ Interacting with others ❑ Told to do something (take a shower, etc) ❑ Something was taken away ❑ Asked to leave a location ❑	❑ picking (lips, fingers, toes) ❑ Self Injury – hitting head or ___ ❑ Hitting others ❑ Kicking ❑ Screaming ❑ crying - Tears? Yes/No	❑ Ignored ❑ Lost privileges (toy/item he had) ❑ Talked to him ("you can't do that" or "let's talk about what happened") ❑ Redirected him ("let's go outside" or "go get your book") ❑ Got what he wanted ❑

ABC Data Sheet Option 1

ABC Data Checklist
STUDENT INITIALS: _____

INITIALS/ DATE:	START & STOP TIME:	LOCATION:	ANTECEDENT: WHAT HAPPENED BEFORE?	BEHAVIOR: WHAT DID IT LOOK LIKE?	CONSEQUENCE: WHAT HAPPENED AFTER?
		☐ CLASSROOM ☐ LUNCHROOM ☐ PLAYGROUND ☐ BATHROOM ☐ HALLWAY ☐ _____	☐ DEMAND GIVEN ☐ DENIED ACCESS ☐ ATTENTION TO OTHER STUDENT ☐ DESK WORK ☐ CIRCLE TIME ☐ WALKING IN HALL ☐ _____	☐ YELLING ☐ CRYING ☐ HITTING ☐ KICKING ☐ VERBAL REFUSAL ☐ PROPERTY DESTRUCTION ☐ _____	☐ DEMAND KEPT ☐ KEPT DENIED ACCESS ☐ ATTENTION REMOVED ☐ _____

ABC Data Sheet Option 2

Scatterplot

Scatterplot is a VERY useful method to measure and graph your data. It is used to determine *when* a problem behavior occurs. Collecting this data may show you that the student's scratching behaviors occur every day at 11:30, during the transition to lunch. This data could lead you to ask more questions or get more information. For example, is it too loud for them in the cafeteria? Are they being bullied by another student?

Name: Dan						**Date: 2/22/21**			
Behavior: Scratching									
	Day 1	Day 2	Day 3	Day 4	Day 5	Day 6	Day 7	Day 8	Day 9
8:00-8:30									
8:30-9:00									
9:00-9:30									
9:30-10:00									
10:00-10:30									
10:30-11:00									
11:00-11:30	X		X	X	X	X	X	X	X
11:30-12:00	X	X	X	X	X	X		X	
12:00-12:30									
12:30-1:00									
1:00-1:30									
1:30-2:00									
2:00-2:30									
2:30-3:00									

Scatterplot Data Sheet for Scratching Behavior

Baseline Data

Taking baseline data is your starting point. It tells us precisely how many times a behavior is occurring BEFORE we do anything to change it. It's valuable because it's specific and measurable and tells us more than "he does it a lot," or "less than before," or our favorite, "it's gotten much better/worse!"

Setting Baseline Criteria

How much baseline data needs to be collected? Generally speaking, you want to take at least three-to-five baseline data points (showing that many instances of behavior). This will show a pattern and tell us if the behavior increases, decreases, or stays reasonably stable.

Example: You want to see how often Tim is late for math class. You decide to track how many times per week he is tardy. Every day when he comes in, you mark how many times per week he is tardy (rate). Your data shows he is late on three out of five days. There are your five baseline data points!

Criteria for Setting Goals

When looking to *decrease* problem behavior, you shouldn't expect a behavior that occurs very often to dramatically reduce from the start. If Zeke pinches sixty times per hour, it would be unreasonable for us to set the first goal to zero. A more appropriate short-term objective may be to reduce pinching to fifty times per hour. Sometimes you will implement something fabulous, and it WILL decrease immediately to zero. More often, you will see a decreasing trend and that's ok, as long as it is headed in the right direction: DOWN.

When looking to *increase* desirable behavior, you also don't want to jump too far ahead. If the baseline shows Hannah is reading six words per minute, you would not set a goal of having her read 100 words per minute. You would start with something more reasonable, let's say ten, and then increase as her skills develop to twenty, thirty, and so on. Setting the criteria too high can set up a student (and teacher) for a lot of unnecessary frustration.

We always want our data to be representative of exactly what we see in the classroom. You may need to enlist your leadership team to help you collect representative data by allowing you to have a paraprofessional come in JUST to take data for a few days. When dealing with behaviors that occur very often, we recognize that taking accurate data can be challenging. Ain't nobody got time for that! Because you already have so much on your plate, you may not have time to sit down with your data sheet and observe. We get that and we are here to help. Listed below are some hacks for data collection.

- Use time sampling methods to get a snapshot of the behavior.
- Keep an index card for each student on a carabiner to carry with you.
- Download a data collection app.
- Use a MotivAider timer to remind you to jot down data at that moment.
- Use pennies or bracelets (or any small objects) to move from one wrist or pocket to another.
- Document multiple students' goals on one data sheet based on the activity.
- Store data sheets where they will be used. For example, bathroom goals in the bathroom, circle time goals on the rug, etc.
- Label your clickers/counters for the specific student or behaviors you are tracking.
- Tie a string around a clipboard and carry it with you.
- Use your phone to take screenshots of your phone's stopwatch so you don't have to keep resetting the time.
- When appropriate, have students take data on themselves!
- Put a piece of painter's tape on your pants or sleeve to document trials as correct (+) or incorrect (-).
- Write on the table with a dry erase marker and take pictures.
- Use golf beads to track frequency.

Graphing

You may be wondering if graphing is really necessary. Absolutely! Why? Let us walk you through a scenario here: You implement an intervention and you measure how many times one student needs to be verbally prompted to turn in his homework. The data points collected are: 3, 3, 4, 1, 4, 3, 5, 1. Are they making any progress? There really is no way to tell until you graph it. By looking at the graph, you are able to see that the data is trending down, meaning that the student is needing less prompts to turn in his homework.

In the ABA world, we love graphs. Providing information in this format will allow a behavior specialist to quickly see how things are going in the classroom. It also will allow an IEP (Individual Education Plan) committee a better understanding of the progress the student has made.

The easiest and fastest way to show this information is with a line graph. There are many free graphing programs available including Microsoft Excel or IPad Numbers and a quick Google search will show you (or your students) how to do so. Be sure to check our Facebook page (Behavior Queens) for examples of this as well!

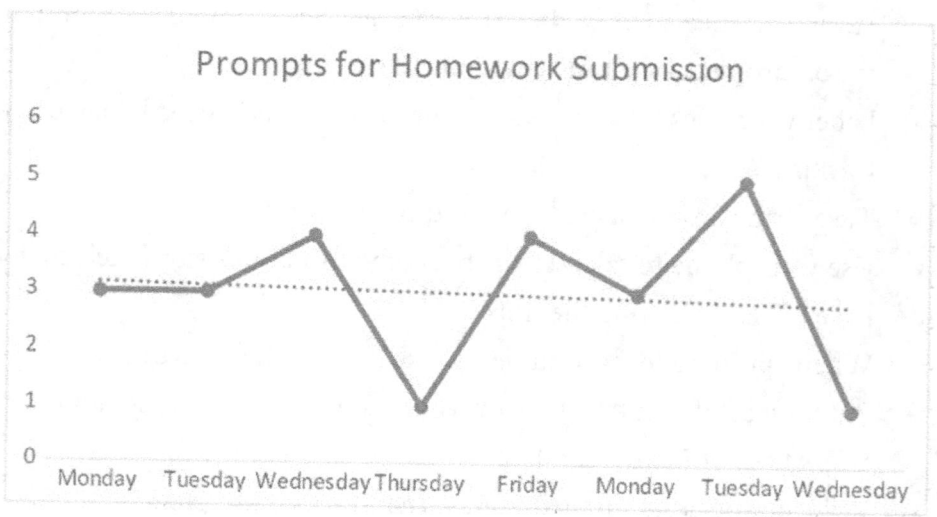

NOTES:

Chapter 4:

This Is NOT A Test!

The Assessment Process

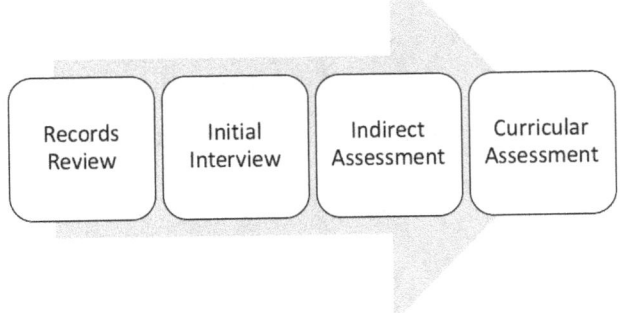

Assessment Process

Assessments are used to determine student's strengths and weaknesses in specific areas and show us how to tailor our instruction. There are several assessments we commonly use when conducting a behavior assessment. The one you choose to use will depend on several factors, including the child's age and stage of development. This process includes a parent interview and an assessment of the areas in which the student has shown delays. Traditionally, this includes:

- Communication
- Self-help skills
- Motor skills
- Social/emotional skills
- Cognitive skills

Records Review

Before beginning work with a student, you will want to review all available records, evaluations, prior IEPs, and other relevant records. This will help you gain a better understanding of the student's history.

Initial Interview

Conduct an initial interview with the parent, caregivers, previous teachers and therapists, and others who spend a significant amount of time with the student. The purpose of this interview is to get a snapshot of the student's strengths and needs, as well as any other relevant information, such as items and activities they like.

Indirect Assessments

FAST

The Functional Analysis Screening Tool (FAST) is a tool that assists in identifying hypothetical causes of problem behaviors. It pinpoints factors that may contribute to problem behaviors and is administered to parents, caregivers, or others who frequently interact with the learner. After completing the twenty-seven question interview, observation of the problem behavior is then conducted to identify possible causes of the behavior.

QABF

The Questions About Behavioral Function (QABF) is an assessment also used to help determine functions of behavior. Consisting of twenty-five items, each question is scored on a Likert-type scale.

Curricular Assessments

VB-MAPP

There are several curricular assessments, including the Verbal Behavior Milestones Assessment and Placement Program (VB-MAPP). This assessment is traditionally used with kids with autism spectrum disorders (ASD) and determines which skills have been mastered and which skills still need to be taught. It focuses mainly on language and challenging behaviors and is used as a curriculum guide and skills tracking system. The VB-MAPP includes five sections:

1. Milestones—Evaluates the student's learning and language skills, including requesting, motor imitation, social play, early academics, etc.
2. Barriers—Evaluates difficulties the student may have, including behavior problems, dependency on prompts, inability to generalize skills, etc.
3. Transitions—Focuses on the student's progress. This section is especially helpful for the IEP teams who need a measurable tool to make educational decisions about the student.
4. Task analysis & skills tracking—Breaks down the skills into steps and can be used as a curriculum guide. This section helps teachers with a variety of activities for teaching students to use new skills in different settings.
5. Placement & IEP goals—Provides specific directions and suggestions on potential objectives.

ABLLS-R

The Assessment of Basic Language and Learning Skills-Revised (ABLLS-R) is another example of an assessment, curriculum guide, and skill-tracking system combo. It, too, focuses on teaching language and learning skills to kids on the spectrum and related developmental disabilities. It addresses:

- Language
- Social interaction
- Motor skills
- Academic skills

While ABLLS-R is traditionally used with children with ASD, it can be used with anyone with delayed communication or life skills. Unlike the VB-MAPP, the ABLLS-R takes significantly longer to assess the over 544 skills from twenty-five skill areas. The assessment results can identify barriers that may contribute to the student's difficulty learning new skills.

AFLS

The Assessment of Functional Living Skills (AFLS) is similar to the ABLLS-R. The AFLS focuses on skills needed to be independent in the home, school, and community settings. It is broken into six individual assessments focusing on the following skills:

- Basic living
- Home
- Community participation
- School
- Independent living
- Vocational

Each assessment can be used individually or in combination to give a complete picture of the student's ability to function independently. It includes a teaching guide with suggestions and strategies.

Superhero Secret:
It's a good idea to reassess every now and then—especially if you see
a new behavior developing. We suggest every six months.

Preference Assessments

Preference assessments are those we complete to identify possible items/activities/people/places the student may find reinforcing. You may already think you know what is reinforcing to them. All kids like candy and praise, right? Wrong. Different things are reinforcing to different people at different times. One kid in your class may love it when you praise them in front of their classmates, while it may be humiliating for another. That student may prefer you to slip them a little note at the end of the day or pull them aside discretely and tell them how proud of them you are. Some students may be embarrassed by getting in trouble in front of the class, while other students may actually love that public reprimand.

How do we select reinforcers? The rule of thumb here is to only select reinforcers if we have evidence that they will increase the behavior in the future. We can start with a simple survey. Ask the kid or their parents/teachers/therapists to complete a preference assessment to identify what items or activities they like. In these surveys and interviews, be sure to think outside of the box by including not only tangible items but also people, places, objects, and activities that they enjoy.

Your survey may look very different depending on the population you work with. In a general education fifth grade class, you may choose to use Survey Monkey or another online tool, and your questions may look something like this:

> **What is your favorite candy?**
>
> **Which one of your classmates is your favorite to hang out with?**
>
> **If you could do silent reading anywhere in the school, where would it be?**
>
> **Do you prefer more computer time or a longer recess?**

For younger students, or those who are unable to read, you may choose to use pictures or interview them.

Preference Assessment for Favorite Candy

After completing an initial survey or interview, you will want to move on to the formal preference assessments: time-based, paired choice, or multiple choice.

A time-based preference assessment is when you observe the student interacting with items in their environment and note how long each interaction occurs. The items are then ranked.

Time-Based Preference Assessment

Student: MM   **Date:** 1/20/2020
Time: 1:05 pm   **Assessor:** Ms. Davis

Item/ Activity	Time Picked Up	Time Put Down	Duration
Firetruck	1:05	1:07	2m
Beads	1:08	1:08	<1m
Firetruck	1:09	1:14	5m
Doll	1:14	1:15	1m
Blocks	1:22	1:23	1m
Firetruck	1:22	1:23	1m
Blocks	1:24	1:30	6m

Preferences:
1. Blocks- 12m
2. Firetruck- 8m
3. Doll- 1m
4. Beads- <1m

Time-Based Preference Assessment

Paired choice, or forced choice, includes presenting the items two at a time and having the child make a choice. You're finished once all items have been paired together. The items are ranked based on the percentage of trials in which they were chosen.

Forced Choice Preference Assessment

Student Name: LaTo   Date: 4/27/20
Teacher: Ms. Pots

A: fidget spinner
B: popit
C: slime
D: playdough

Trial	Item Selected
1	A (B)
2	(C) A
3	(A) D
4	B (C)
5	D (B)
6	(C) D

Results:

A selected _1_ times
B selected _2_ times
C selected _3_ times
D selected _0_ times

Paired Choice Preference Assessment

Multiple choice with replacement is when you place a series of items in front of the child. After the child chooses an item, you add it back into the array and shuffle all of the items.

Multiple Stimulus with Replacement

Student: RP   Date: 4-1-21
Assessor: Ms. Davis   Time: 9:10am

Items:

A. Skittles	E. Pretzel
B. Bubbles	F. Car
C. Slime	G. Book
D. Ball	H. Cracker

A	B	C	D	E	F	G	H
B	C	D	E	F	G	H	A
C	D	E	F	G	H	A	B
D	E	F	G	H	A	B	C
E	F	G	H	A	B	C	D
F	G	H	A	B	C	D	E
G	H	A	B	C	D	E	F
H	A	B	C	D	E	F	G

Preferences:

1. skittle- 37.4%	5.
2. slime- 37.5%	6.
3. pretzel- 12.5%	7.
4. car- 12.5%	

Multiple Stimulus with Replacement of Items

Multiple choice without replacement occurs when you do not replace the item after it is chosen. In round one, you may start with seven items, and the student will select one. In round two, you will have six items, and so on. All of the items are ranked.

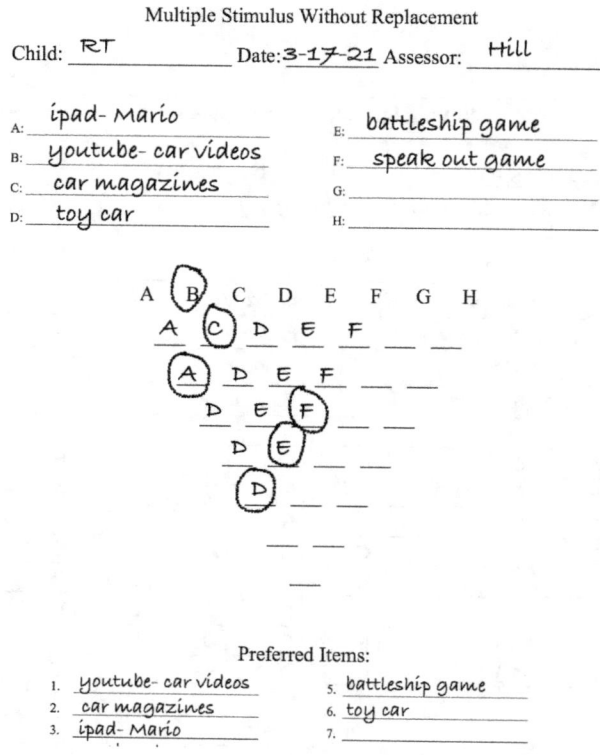

Multiple Stimulus Without Replacement

Child: RT _____ Date: 3-17-21 Assessor: Hill _____

A: ipad- Mario
B: youtube- car videos
C: car magazines
D: toy car
E: battleship game
F: speak out game
G: _____
H: _____

Preferred Items:
1. youtube- car videos
2. car magazines
3. ipad- Mario
4.
5. battleship game
6. toy car
7.

Multiple Stimulus Without Replacement of Items

Types of Preference Assessments	Pros	Cons
Time-Based (AKA Free-Operant)	• You are able to see automatic behavior	• Time consuming • Can't see how the item selected compares to other items

Natalie L. Perkel, Ph.D., BCBA & Beverly G. Smith, M.Ed., BCBA, LBA

Forced Choice (AKA Paired Choice)	• Good for students who are unable to scan a large group or those who have a hard time making choices	• Time Consuming • Must remove the items from the student once selected to continue assessment
Multiple stimulus with replacement	• Allows you to see how the items are ranked • Gives you information on how quickly the learner loses interest in a specific reinforcer	• Need multiple items to choose from • Must remove the items from the student once selected to continue assessment
Multiple stimulus without replacement	• Allows you to see how the items are ranked	• Need multiple items to choose from • Must remove the items from the student once selected to continue assessment

Preference assessments should be completed at the beginning of the school year and repeated periodically throughout the school year. Think about it—don't your preferences change from time to time? Well, it's the same with your students! Keep in mind that just because your student prefers an item doesn't mean they'll be motivated to work for it or that it will change their behavior. As you implement strategies, your data will show you if the items you selected as preferences are indeed changing the behaviors (which means they really are reinforcers by definition.) If the behavior is NOT changing, it may be a good idea to revisit the items that were identified in the preference assessment and try something different.

Superhero Secret:

We can get a good idea of the things that motivate our students by doing a preference assessment. Just because you think something is reinforcing to them doesn't mean it really is! Ask their parents, conduct formal preference assessments, and observe them. Keep trying until you find something they're willing to work for!

Here are a few tips to remember when determining what reinforces your students:

1. Be persistent—everyone is reinforced by something. You get to figure out what that is!
2. Use your resources—ask the student, parents, and other individuals who work with the student to identify items and activities.
3. Conduct preference assessments often—preferences change.
4. Limit/restrict access to those reinforcers to encourage more motivation when needed.

Challenges with Identifying Reinforcers

Problem- "Nothing reinforces the student."

Solution- Reframe the question. Instead of asking the parent/teacher/therapist to identify reinforcers, ask the following questions:

1. **What do they like to do?**
2. **What foods do they like to eat?**
3. **What toys do they like to play with?**
4. **Are there any items they can't live without?**
5. **Are there any behaviors they often engage in?**
6. **Who is their favorite person?**

7. Where do they like to go?
8. When are they happiest?

Problem- "It's not working anymore."

Solution- We love chocolate. But if we have access to chocolate all day long, we're probably going to need a break from it (theoretically, anyhow). It's important to vary your reinforcers and limit access to favorite items and activities so they remain motivating.

<u>NOTES:</u>

Natalie L. Perkel, Ph.D., BCBA & Beverly G. Smith, M.Ed., BCBA, LBA

Chapter 5:

Behavior Junction, What's the Function?

Functions of Behavior

All behavior serves some kind of purpose. We engage in different behaviors to communicate one of four needs:

- Attention
- Escape
- Access to tangibles (to get something we want)
- Automatic (because we like it, or it meets some sensory need)

Think about this for a second...ALL BEHAVIOR.

Why did you just smile at that fireman? To get his attention. Why did you make a second batch of cinnamon rolls? Because they taste amazing. Why did you rush through your lesson plans tonight? To get them over with so you can watch Netflix.

It's important to identify the function (purpose) of a behavior because people may engage in the EXACT same behavior for different reasons. See the examples below:

- *Vivian screamed at the top of her lungs because she wanted to get your attention.*

- *Lily screamed at the top of her lungs because she doesn't want to do any more of her math worksheet.*

- *Jake screamed at the top of his lungs because he wanted to have the toy Vivian has.*

- *Jim screamed at the top of his lungs because he likes the vibration in his throat.*

Each time, the behavior looks exactly the same, but the reason behind the scream is what makes it different. Why is this important? The intervention you implement will need to match the function. It must meet the same need as the problem behavior. Let's break this down:

Vivian's scream was clearly to get your undivided attention. There are certainly other ways to do so, and she may need to be taught another way. Teaching her to raise her hand, how to say, "excuse me," or having her walk over to you may be some options that would get her the attention she seeks without engaging in any problem behaviors.

Lily screamed to get out of an activity she was doing. In this example, the function is escape. Teaching Lily how to ask for a break may be all she needs to prevent the screaming.

Jake's screaming appeared to have happened because he wanted something someone else has. Therefore, in this situation, the function of the behavior is to gain access. In this case, we may need to teach Jake how to ask for something that he wants in a more socially acceptable way or to learn to wait.

Jim liked the way screaming felt. We refer to this sensory experience as automatic reinforcement, and we may teach Jim to gargle with water to get the same vibration.

BEHAVIOR JUNCTION, WHAT'S THE FUNCTION?

As you can see in the examples above, many behaviors can be changed by teaching a more appropriate response. Individuals learn (sometimes through years of engaging in a specific problem behavior) that behaviors get needs met, and that's what they'll do to keep getting what they want. In the examples above, we provided replacement behaviors. These are just what they sound like—preferred behaviors that will take the place of the undesired behaviors (screaming, in this case).

Superhero Secret:
When addressing problem behaviors, we first need to determine the function. If you use a one-size-fits-all approach to handling behaviors, the behaviors are just going to continue (and possibly increase!).

THE PROBLEM: Many people hear the screaming and JUST WANT IT TO STOP. If we treat each of the above situations the same, we will not stop the behavior. For example, all the attention in the world isn't going to satisfy Jake—he doesn't want your attention; he wants THE THING. You can give Vivian a new toy to play with, but ultimately, it's you that she wants, and until she gets your attention, she's going to keep screaming.

We want to give you a nifty way to remember the four functions to drive home their significance. Yep, they are THAT important.

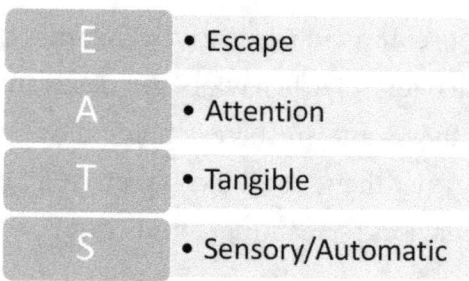

You may be thinking: How do you identify the function? Remember in the last section we talked about collecting ABC data, using the FAST, and/or the QABF? Bingo! Information from those assessments will allow you to hypothesize the purpose of your student's behavior. Identifying the function will help us decide the best way to move forward and select the most effective treatment. You will look in the consequence column of your ABC data sheet to get this information.

For example:

- If the consequence consistently shows that the student receives attention after they engage in behavior X, you can hypothesize the function is attention.
- If the consequence shows that the student gets out of doing a task, you can hypothesize the function is escape.
- If the consequence shows that the student engages in the problem behavior after an item or activity is removed, you can hypothesize the function is access to tangible.
- If the consequence shows that the student engages in the behavior throughout the day, in all settings, even when no one is around, you can hypothesize the function is automatic/sensory.

Often, when trying to address behaviors, we put all of our energy into focusing on the "symptoms"—the specific behaviors we are seeing, and we use a one-size-fits-all approach. For instance, we've been in classrooms before where the teacher responded to all problem behaviors (talking out, yelling, cheating, not paying attention, getting out of their seats, etc.) with reprimands. Every problem behavior was met with the teacher raising her voice and telling the student to stop doing the behavior. Other times, we have gone into classrooms and the teachers responded to all behaviors with using "time-out" or using a behavior chart. There is no analysis of *why* the behavior is occurring or if the choice of a reprimand is indeed the correct response to the behavior. In those situations, we love to help the teacher recognize that behaviors they are seeing are just the tip of an iceberg—there is so much below the surface that we need to discover and evaluate in order to truly address the behavior. When we dive in and explore the student's history, medical issues, the antecedents, patterns in the behavior, and environmental events, then we are able to take an educated approach and respond in a manner that is actually going to be effective in reducing the behavior in the future.

<u>NOTES:</u>

Natalie L. Perkel, Ph.D., BCBA & Beverly G. Smith, M.Ed., BCBA, LBA

Chapter 6:

Stop in the Name of ABA!

Prevention Strategies

Teachers are pros when it comes to preventative strategies, many times without realizing it! We pack fidget toys for field trips, put permanent markers or scissors out of reach, and separate best friends to prevent them from talking. By changing what happens before the problem behavior begins, we can often prevent those behaviors from occurring in the first place.

Superhero Secret:
We always tell teachers to only give a demand if they are able to follow through. If you are tired, sick, or short-handed, you are much more likely to give in after a few minutes of whining. While this isn't ideal, save the tough stuff for when you are well and rested.

Eight prevention strategies are:

1. Avoid taking your students to certain places or around certain people. For example, you may not take students to a pep rally if they are sensitive to loud noises.

2. Make changes in the environment. For example, seat young students in chairs at circle time to prevent them from moving around on the rug.

3. Do things in small steps. For example, reserve the library, so your class doesn't have to wait in line for as long at the book fair.

4. Change the order of activities. This strategy is especially helpful for kiddos who have difficulty with transitions. Instead of having the child stop playing with their iPad to go to the bathroom, you can make the iPad contingent on going to the bathroom. Tell the student, "First go to the bathroom, then you can play on your iPad for two minutes."

5. Respond to early signs of problem behaviors. Teachers may pick up on "red flag" behaviors: those behaviors that occur before the problem behaviors. For example, a student may suddenly become very whiny or may begin to rub their eyes and yawn. If you pick up on these early signs before they bite their classmate, you may decide to give them a break BEFORE they have a meltdown.

6. Change the demand or response. One example of changing the demand is instead of saying "Tony, do your worksheet," saying "Tony, do you want to do your worksheet in pen or pencil?" Similarly, you could change the response. Does your student become agitated anytime they hear the word "no?" One solution is to avoid the word altogether and instead offer choices. An example of changing your response is instead of saying "No, you can't have your iPad," saying "You can have a book or color right now." Sometimes changing how we ask or respond to our students can prevent problem behaviors.

7. Address setting events. Setting events are things that can affect the child's at-school behaviors, such as being sick, hungry, or sleepy. Let's say you have a student who is always starving when they arrive at school. You could talk with their parents about making sure they are eating breakfast or offer them a snack when they get to school in the morning.

8. Visual and auditory cues can be used to prevent problem behaviors. You can post a visual schedule in the classroom to show the students what activities will occur that day or play the clean-up song a few minutes before it's time to change activities.

Superhero Secret:
If your student is hungry, tired, sick, or experiencing medication changes, you may want to reconsider introducing something new or giving them difficult demands. Changes in the environment are another exception. Is it a holiday? Do they have family in town visiting? This may not be the best time to introduce handwriting or some other complex skill.

Priming (Preparing)

Priming is a strategy that is especially helpful for students who have difficulty with transitions or new situations. With priming, we introduce things to the student ahead of time to help them know what is coming next. By doing so, we familiarize them with changes in their schedule or new situations that may occur. Some ways to prime students for changes are through the use of visuals, timers, watching videos, role-playing, and schedules. It may be as easy as saying, "Ok class, in five minutes we will finish up language arts and start math," or it may be more involved, such as touring the new school the student will attend the following year. We can make priming even more effective by combining new environments or people with positive experiences and reinforcement.

Pairing

When educators discuss prepping for the first days of school with new students, there is a considerable focus on setting expectations. "Let the kids know what you expect from them," they say. This is very different than the first few days of working with a student using ABA. We always start with pairing.

What is pairing? Pairing is building trust and respect with your student. Basically, you want the kid to fall in love with you. "What?! Why do I need the kid to love me? I don't need to be their friend—I'm their teacher. They'll eventually love me as the year goes on." Any of these thoughts going through your head right now?

You want the kid to love you to make your life easier. Trust us on this one. You don't just want your student to sit in the chair. You want them to *want* to sit in the chair. You don't just want your student to do the worksheet. You want them to *want* to do the worksheet. If you are effectively paired with your student, then they will want to work for you. They will enjoy being around you and will realize that you are the gateway to reinforcement.

Superhero Secret:
In addition to people, you can pair places, activities, and objects.

Pairing occurs when you combine a preferred item/activity/person with an unpreferred item/activity/person. When you do this, the characteristics of the preferred "thing" transfers to the unpreferred "thing" and now we like it!

Maybe your student hates reading or math...pair it with a reinforcer.

Maybe they don't like taking turns or eating in the cafeteria...pair it!

Step One:

Figure out what reinforcers you will use. Look back at preference assessments you have completed to get ideas on this.

Step Two:

Be upbeat, fun, and provide endless reinforcement. You heard us. Endless. We often hear teachers say, "But I don't want the kid to become dependent on candy as a reinforcer" or "They will begin to expect constant reinforcement." We're not asking you to do this forever—just in the beginning.

If you move on without being effectively paired, teaching new skills and changing behavior will be much more difficult. So put on your Oprah hat and start passing out the good stuff: "YOU get a Skittle and YOU get a high five and YOU ARE AMAZING!"

Step Three:

Look at areas in which your student demonstrates problem behavior. Can you introduce that person/activity/item while incorporating something they like? Let's look at a couple of real-world examples to get a better idea of this concept.

Zoe hates silent reading. She disturbs her classmates by making silly noises the whole time. But Zoe loves music. You can pair silent reading with listening to music to make it a more enjoyable activity.

Every day during recess, Anju only plays on the slide and refuses to play any other activities. She must go up and down that thing at least 100 times. Try pairing swinging with her best friend by having them swing next to each other in order to expand leisure activities.

Step Four:

Once you have effectively paired a favorable activity with a less favorable activity, you can fade out the more preferred activity. Zoe won't have to listen to music during silent reading forever and Anju will eventually swing without her best friend. You won't have to constantly give away high fives and Skittles indefinitely. When you have had consistent success, start fading it. Slowly. Maybe allow some time to go by without reinforcement, provide a smaller amount of reinforcement, or require the student to do more to earn it. The best practice is to take data here and slowly fade the reinforcers.

Instructional Control

At the beginning of every school year, you will need to establish your role as the class leader. Below is a step-by-step guide to assist in helping to create productive working relationships.

1. Let your student see that you are in charge of fun, desirable items and activities.
2. Pair yourself with the student.
3. Show the student that you will do what you say you will do.
4. Let the student see how they will benefit from following directions.
5. When learning a new task or skill, reinforce every response.
6. Use information from preference assessments to identify what the child likes most.
7. Let the student see that participating in undesirable behaviors will not allow them to access reinforcers.

Prompting

It's kind of a miracle teachers don't lose their voices more often, as it's basically a teacher's job to talk non-stop all day long. Can we get an Amen? Some teachers make one BIG mistake—they constantly prompt their students, and the students begin to depend on the prompts instead of completing the tasks independently.

What is a prompt? A prompt is something we add before a behavior occurs in order to elicit that preferred behavior.

Let's look at an example here: After Antonio finishes using the bathroom, you walk him over to the sink, and he stands waiting for you to tell him what to do next. With you prompting him through hand washing, he can complete each step. Your job there is done because the task has been completed, right? WRONG! For a skill to truly be considered independent, the student needs to complete it without any additional assistance.

There are two main types of prompts: stimulus prompts and response prompts. Stimulus prompts occur when you use movement, position, or redundancy to bring about the correct response.

Types of Stimulus Prompts	Uses	Examples
Movement	Tapping, pointing to, touching, or looking at the correct answer.	When teaching letters, you put three letters in front of your students and ask them to touch the letter D while you are tapping the letter at the same time.

Position	Positioning the correct answer closer to the student.	When teaching identifying animals, you place two animal pictures on the table and ask your student to identify the cat while positioning the picture of the cat closer to her.
Redundancy	Using more than one feature to indicate the correct answer.	When teaching colors, you hold up two color words and ask the student to point to the word yellow which is also written in a yellow font.

Response prompts occur when you use words, pictures, or actions to encourage the correct response. You are probably using some of these already!

There are four main types of response prompts:

1. A **verbal** prompt is what you *say* to the learner when teaching a new skill. This may be giving a hint, stressing a particular word, or giving part of the answer. For example, you may ask, "What color is this? It starts with the sound /p/" or "Who was the first President of the U.S.? His last name is also the name of a state."

2. A **visual** prompt is "something" your student *sees* when learning a new skill. Everyone uses visual prompts. Traffic signs, post-it notes, gestures, visual schedules, visual timers, and other pictures are examples of visual prompts that we use often.

3. A **modeling** prompt is "something" you *show* the student to teach a new skill. They are learning how to do the skill by watching and then imitating you. Children often learn from modeling after their peers. Imitating may come

naturally for one student but may be more difficult for others. In this case, you need to teach them EXACTLY how to imitate.

4. A **physical** prompt is when you *physically* guide the student to complete the correct response (ex. cutting with scissors or writing their name.) Physical prompts can fall anywhere on a scale from partial physical guidance (such as tapping their elbow) to full physical guidance (such as placing your hands on their hands and picking up a pen). Many teachers refer to full-physical guidance as hand-over-hand prompting. As the child becomes more independent, you can back off.

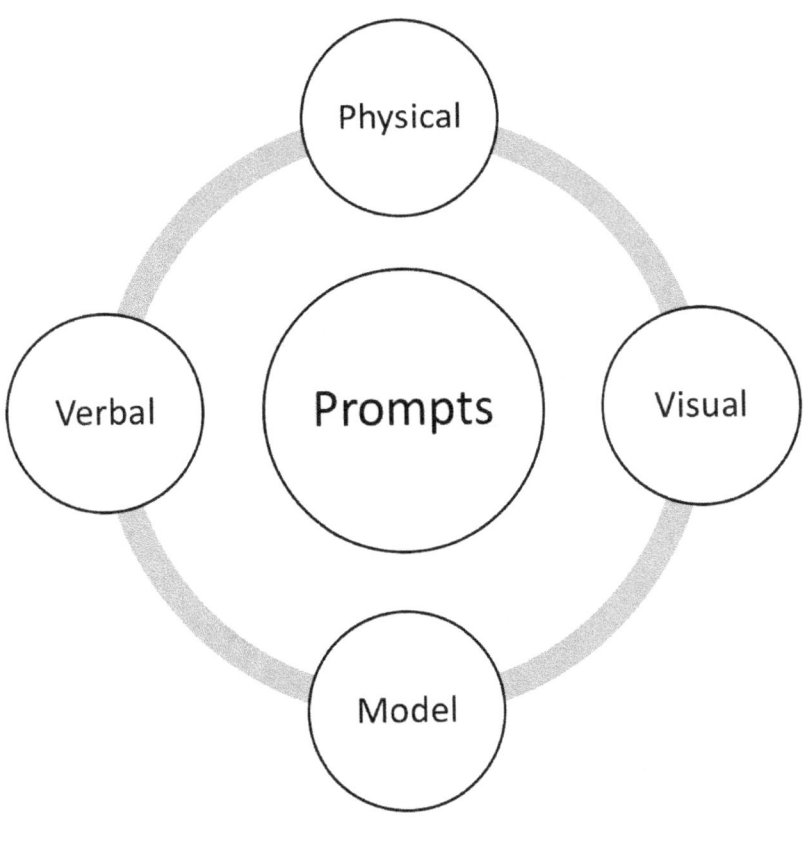

Types of Prompts

Prompt Recommendations

- **Identify how much of the task the student can complete independently to know how much support they will need.**
- **Use only the prompting level required for the child to be successful, <u>no more</u>.**
- **Use a variety of prompts to teach a skill.**
- **Add or remove prompts as needed and remember to remove them as quickly as you are able.**
- **Prompt certain parts of a series of skills.**

Our goal is to teach our students to complete tasks independently instead of us telling/showing/helping them every step of the way. There are four ways in which we do this.

1. The first is most-to-least prompting. With this procedure, you gradually reduce the amount of assistance provided each time you practice the skill. You may start with physically guiding the child and then using a picture (visual prompt), before only using vocal instructions (verbal prompt), and finally not using any prompts (independence!).

The teacher started by taking Antonio's hands in their hands and completing each step of the handwashing process. The next time, they moved their hands back to his elbows and lightly assisted him. Then, the teacher moved to using pictures of each step while sometimes providing some physical assistance if he paused for more than five seconds. Once he consistently followed the steps, the teacher moved to just the vocal instructions. Again, if he got stuck, they would pull out one of the visuals to show him what to do next. Finally, Antonio was able to wash his hands all by himself without the teacher's help at all.

2. Secondly, we can use graduated guidance to fade prompts. With this procedure, you only add prompts on the steps where they are needed.

The teacher gradually increases the distance by moving from full-physical to lightly touching Antonio's elbows. The teacher can jump back in and provide a full-physical prompt if needed.

3. The third prompt fading procedure is called least-to-most. This is basically the opposite of most-to-least prompting. The teacher allows the student a brief window of time to respond independently, and if they do not, the teacher steps in and provides the smallest prompt needed for the correct response.

The teacher waits a few seconds for Antonio to turn the water on before saying, "turn on the water." If he still doesn't, they may show him a visual, lightly guide his elbow toward the faucet, tap the faucet, or model turning it on.

4. The final prompt fading procedure is referred to as time-delay. With this procedure, you wait before prompting the student.

At first, the teacher gives Antonio the direction to wash his hands while immediately prompting him. There is no delay between the instruction and the prompt. They will then move to a three-second delay before slowly increasing the time increments until Antonio is completing the steps independently.

So what's the takeaway here? Prompts are great! They are incredibly effective when teaching new skills and can be a great resource in the classroom. Prompts can aid your students in learning a new task without becoming frustrated. They can also prevent your students from learning a skill the wrong way. Before using them, it is important that you already have an idea in mind for how you plan to fade them out. It is just as important that you don't fade them out too quickly. You want to make sure that your student is being successful and still coming in contact with rewards.

Non-Contingent Reinforcement (NCR)

Non-contingent reinforcement sounds fancy. The non-contingent part just means that it's free. Free reinforcement! It's technically a preventative strategy, and once you know how to do it, it is incredibly easy to implement. Have you ever been with a group of kids and you say something complimentary to one of them? All of a sudden, EVERYONE is saying, "look at *my* shirt, it's cool too!" or "do you want to know *my* name?!" This is part of the magic behind NCR. Research shows that when you purposefully provide attention to an individual, they are less likely to engage in problem behaviors to get what they want. The reason why it is suspected to work so well is that the individual is getting so much of what they want throughout the day, the behaviors no longer serve a purpose. This is a very common procedure to use when the student is engaging in non-dangerous behaviors. There are three different types of non-contingent reinforcement.

1. NCR with positive reinforcement (or social praise/attention):

Kelly constantly sings during times when the class is silently reading. When she does this, everyone gives her looks or tells her to be quiet. She continues to sing. To use NCR with Kelly, you would provide her with praise throughout the class. For example, when your timer goes off, you would make eye contact with her and smile, say something positive like "I like those boots!" or "do you want to pass this out to the class?" (if that is something she likes to do). You could give her a thumbs up and a smile. Notice that the attention you give is NOT dependent on her behavior. It's TOTALLY free.

2. NCR with negative reinforcement (escape):

Belle regularly puts her head down on her desk during the science lesson when she loses interest. By doing this, she avoids doing her work in class. To provide NCR for Belle, we would remove the lesson BEFORE she puts her head down. We would say something like, "you can have a little break," and give her time without the assignment. A few minutes later, re-present the task and say, "let's try again." By doing this, you avoid the problem behavior by giving frequent breaks and preventing her from losing interest.

3. NCR with automatic reinforcement (sensory):

Bert gets antsy and starts to wiggle in his seat. To prevent this, you have him select an item/activity from his choice board each hour, such as carrying heavy books or rocking in the rocking chair.

Superhero Secret:
Remember to reinforce replacement behaviors BEFORE undesired behavior occurs to ensure that you don't reinforce that undesired behavior.

Behavioral Momentum

"My class is consistently late making it out to the bus at the end of the school day. I just can't get everyone packed up and ready to go in time!"

"The majority of my class transitions back to their desks after circle time when I ask, but I always have a couple of students who move at a snail's pace and delay my teaching."

"I have one student who is just so defiant! I swear, even if they like the activity, they're going to refuse just because I ask them to do it."

Can you relate to any of the above statements we've heard from teachers? If you have similar complaints, you aren't alone. Using behavioral momentum may be just what you need!

If you know your student is less likely to complete a particular task, start with a few quick, easy requests they are likely to do. This way, they will build momentum to complete the task you really want them to do. Are you thinking that sounds a little silly? Well, it's science, and it works!

Look at how you currently do things: you give the student a series of tasks they don't like to do ("do the worksheet," "clean up around your desk," etc.), and they refuse. Maybe they move extra slowly, or they chat with their friend next to them, or they straight up physically refuse by walking out of the room. Maybe they even flop on the floor or act out aggressively. Regardless, the cycle has started, and they're not completing what you asked them to do. There is an easier way.

By taking just a few moments before giving the demand you really want, you can prevent non-compliance from occurring. First, give a few (three-to-five) quick, easy requests you know they commonly complete. After they complete those tasks and the momentum is building, give the non-desired task.

Here are a couple of examples:

While at circle time:
Teacher: *"Clap your hands. Great! Stand up. Perfect! Give your neighbor a high five. That's it! Walk quickly to your seats."*

At the end of centers:
Teacher: *"Touch your nose. Good! Look at me. Nice! Smile. Beautiful! Clean up your center."*

See how that works? It's pretty cool, right? It's one of those things that you have to see to believe!

When using behavioral momentum, there are a few things you'll want to keep in mind:

1. The first three-to-five tasks need to be mastered. These are things that the student can already do easily. Think simple, fun, fast tasks.

2. Be sure to reward those first simple tasks. You want the student to be rewarded for completing those easy tasks to get the behavioral momentum rolling.

3. Behavioral momentum is used to prevent problem behavior. This isn't a tool you want to pull out after problem behavior starts. If you wait until the student starts screaming or flops on the floor to use this, you could accidentally reinforce that behavior. So be sure to plan ahead!

Classroom Setup

There you are: standing in your brand-new classroom. Perhaps you have access to a ton of fabulous furniture, the newest technology, and the most popular manipulatives and materials. Maybe you don't have any of that. Or, maybe you're a veteran teacher and you are just looking for a few tweaks to your classroom environment to better support your students. Wherever you are, we are here to help! We've developed an easy peasy three-step method for setting up your classroom.

Superhero Secret:
Setting up your classroom effectively is a great antecedent strategy
that can actually prevent problem behaviors from occurring.

Step 1—Plan

Would you start building your house without having a blueprint? Heck no! Planning out your classroom structure, schedules, centers, and activities are vital to your students' ability to be successful. We recommend starting with your schedule. First, look at the school schedule and fill in any "mandatory" events like the start and end of the school day, lunch times, and any enrichment times, recess, etc. From there you will fill in your instructional times. This will need to be individualized to your class based on your students' age and abilities. For example, an elementary self-contained classroom may have a very short whole-group circle time and then rotate through centers for the majority of the day (play area, fine motor with a paraprofessional, discrete trial teaching session with the teacher, computer area, etc.). On the other hand, a high-school resource class may include a lot of transitioning to general education classrooms. One thing you want to keep in mind is to be sure not to schedule reinforcing activities right before difficult or aversive activities. Trust us here. It is much easier to transition from algebra to outside break time than vice versa.

Once you get all of the activities and times filled in, be sure to list who is responsible for each activity and which students will participate in that activity. You may have yourself listed as teaching circle time while Para one is assigned to provide physical prompting to Johnny and Para two is assigned to take Ally to kindergarten math. We like to call this scheduling Jenga. It can feel overwhelming at times but ensuring that you know what is happening at every second of the day and who is responsible for what is going to pay off in the long run.

Step 2—Physical Structure
After completing your schedule (that will change five million times before the end of the year), you are ready to plan the physical structure of the classroom. This, too, will vary greatly based on the age and level of your students. Some common areas we see in classrooms are:

- Circle time
- Small groups
- Individual work areas

- Workstations
- Computer
- Discrete trial teaching area
- Teacher/para desk
- Leisure
- Play
- Reading
- Fine motor
- Sensory

Look at each area that you decide to include and think about potential problem behaviors that could arise so that you can ensure antecedent strategies are in place. For example, let's say you have a student who often elopes. It probably isn't the best idea to put the unsupervised leisure center right next to the door as you don't want to have to constantly chase them down the hall. You may decide to forego having a teacher's desk to have more space or put the student seat at the discrete trial teaching area with their back against the wall to discourage them from getting up. Get creative here!

Step 3—Visual Structure

The final step for setting up your classroom is to use visual structure to set your students up for success! Start with using visual structure to define areas of your classroom. Use bookshelves, room dividers, or anything else you have on hand (hello, painter's tape!) to section off the different areas so that students understand where they are supposed to be during each activity. Often, other teachers are giving away unwanted shelves or other furniture at the beginning and end of each year—keep your eye out to snag those goodies!

Signs are great for labeling the areas, and visuals let the students know what activities are appropriate for that area and remind them of appropriate behaviors. You can find more ideas for visual supports in chapter seven.

One final suggestion—remember to be flexible. If the layout you designed just isn't working, change it! If you realize you are missing visuals in the reading center, then add them! Your classroom is going to always be a work in progress—and that's ok. Our students are constantly changing, and it only makes sense that our classrooms will as well.

NOTES:

Chapter 7:

Show Me!

Visuals

Visuals in the classroom serve as reminders or help us teach new skills. You may have a schedule set in place so that students know what to expect throughout the school day or during the lesson you are teaching. Depending on your student's developmental level, you may write a list of activities on the board, use pictures only, or use a combination of words and pictures. Some of the more popular visuals in classrooms include schedules, menu or choice boards, and flipbooks. Other options may include charts, lists, contracts, calendars, or pictures.

---

10 Tips for Using Visuals

- Visuals can teach new skills such as how to tie your shoes or how to solve a math problem.
- They can be one-step or multiple-step directions such as a sticky note that says, "don't forget your coat!" or a series of pictures showing how to put your coat on.

- They can support different concepts we are teaching, such as "I before E except after C," or the alphabet posted on the wall.
- They provide extra support without singling out specific students. When using visuals, you can silently provide as little of a prompt as necessary to help the student succeed.
- You can teach students to make their own!
- They remind us of the things we forget! ("Oh, that's right, I have that meeting after school...")
- Visuals are reusable, saving you time and effort.
- They can be beneficial when an individual is upset, and you need to keep vocal communication to a minimum.
- You should introduce and explain each visual in detail BEFORE problem behaviors occur. This ensures the student will be familiar with its meaning and use it as needed.
- They can be individualized.

Schedules

Visual schedules are easy to use and can prevent problem behaviors. Yes, it does take some planning to create these. Yes, it does take time and materials. The good news is—the payoff is much bigger than the time and effort you will exert. Visual schedules help the student to know what is coming next, alert them to any schedule changes, and can also save you from having to answer five million questions about the next activity or step. They can reduce the anticipation of the unknown and increase independence. You probably use a schedule yourself—whether on your phone, in a planner, or jotting down a to-do list on a post-it note. Visuals help everyone!

When developing a visual schedule, there are several questions to ask yourself:

1. Who is your audience? Is it the whole class, a group of students, or an individual student? Are they able to read words or understand pictures?

Would they benefit from seeing a full-day schedule or just a few steps at a time?

2. What does a typical day look like? What are any behavioral concerns that occur during the day?

Here are some suggestions for using visual schedules:

- Teach the schedule beforehand by introducing and explaining each picture one at a time
- You may keep a particular student's schedule on their desk or the group schedule on the board
- Encourage your students to check it as needed
- After the student completes an activity, remind them to return to the visual schedule (if needed)
- Discuss any changes in the schedule for the day

Superhero Secret:
Use visual schedules to increase your student's independence (and decrease the number of times they call your name!)

First/Then Chart

The first/then chart is used when we need to simplify a schedule. The basic concept behind a first/then chart is to show the student: FIRST, you will do what I want (their undesired or less desired activity) and THEN you can do what you want (the desired activity). It's also a tool that we can use when we need to simplify a schedule; for example, if Suzie is having a tough day following directions, showing her only one step at a time may be more manageable.

Examples of a first/ then chart in action:

FIRST, complete the worksheet and THEN you can have five minutes on the iPad
FIRST, finish yesterday's classwork and THEN you can do an activity of your choice

These show in a short, concise way both the demand and the upcoming reward. Everyone wins!

First/ Then Chart

Superhero Secret:
Remember, the things we want/like/enjoy change regularly and our students may want something different each day!

Menu Boards/Choice Boards

This is precisely what it sounds like! Imagine you are at a restaurant and the menu only has one item to choose from. You wouldn't be very happy, would you? No! We like options and so do our students.

Menu boards and choice boards give students options to choose from, such as different items, activities, or materials. They can have as few as two selections, for those who have a more difficult time making a choice, or multiple options for learners who can choose from an array. The student can point to what they want, pick it up and move it to another part of the board, or vocally say their selection. You can also use it in conjunction with a first/then board where you take the chosen reward and move it to the "then" part of the first/then chart.

What do you want to choose?

Menu Board for Preferred Activities

Flip Pics

You can use flip pics or flip books in a variety of ways. They serve as a collection of visual prompts for students. Let's say Rashad is having a hard time staying seated during circle time. He may need reminders to:

1. Stay seated and on the rug.
2. Keep his hands to himself.
3. Stay quiet while you are teaching.

The pictures may look like this:

You can bind them together like a little book or punch a hole in them and put the pictures on a binder ring. You can keep them handy to use as needed in certain parts of the classroom or wear them on a lanyard, depending on how often you use them!

When Rashad starts to squirm and move about, you can hold up that visual (without saying anything) and continue your teaching. It's simple, effective, and doesn't affect the flow of instruction.

Timers

Who loves timers? We do! They can give a clear start and end to a task and help those who struggle with transitions. They are great for teaching independence and can be used in punishment protocols such as time out. (Be sure to read the section on time out before using this!)

If you are only using the timer to count down and end fun activities, you are going to have students who form an aversion to them. You will want to be sure to alternate using it at the beginning and end of those activities. For example, you may use one to show Mickey how much time she has left on the computer before doing her science worksheet, and at another time to show how much time she has before recess.

Token Economy

A token system is an easy and manageable way to reward behaviors without disruption. Let's say you have a student who is super motivated by computer time. You can give Jeannie a token for following directions during science, and at the end of the lesson, if she earns all ten tokens, she is able to play on the computer for five minutes. That is much more practical than interrupting the science lesson to play on the computer.

Maybe your kiddo struggles with their reading homework and is really motivated by music. For every page they read, they get a sticker. Once they get five stickers, they get to listen to their favorite song before going back to reading.

Token Economy for Ten Tasks

When using a token economy, there are a few things you want to remember:

1. Deliver tokens immediately and often.
2. Provide verbal praise when delivering the token.
3. Make sure that the kid actually wants the reinforcer they're working for.
4. Don't take away tokens—keep it a positive experience!

You can quickly and easily make your own token economy using a post-it note and stickers, drawing stars on a piece of construction paper, or velcroing poker chips to a ruler. Students working on self-management skills can complete their own token economy. You can add their favorite movie or cartoon character. You can make this as fun or as simple as you'd like.

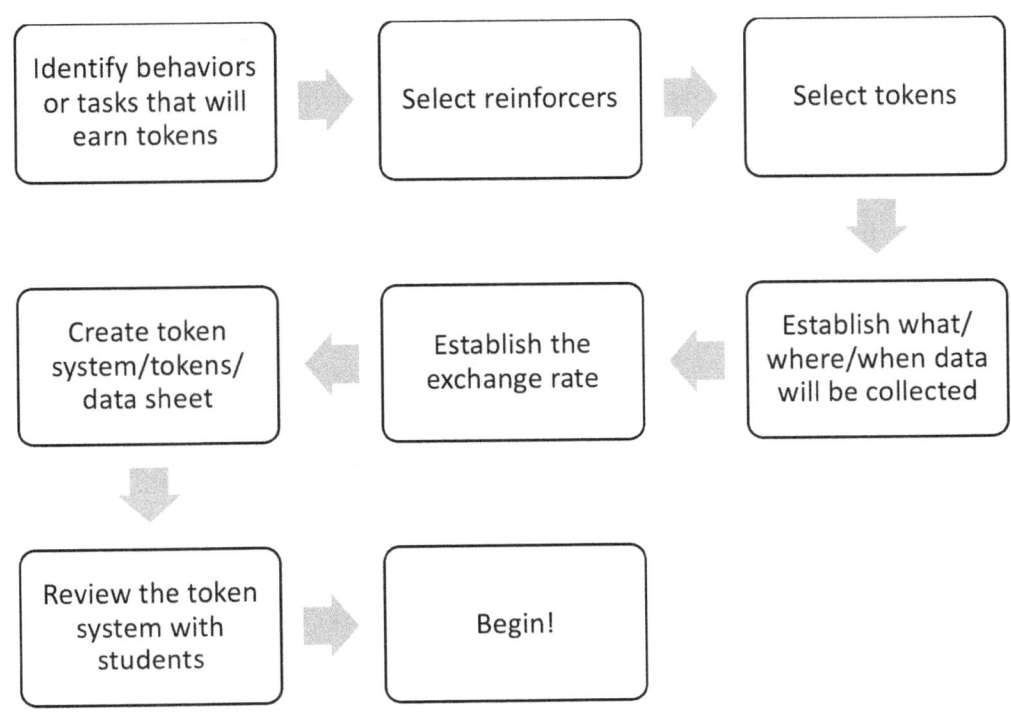

Token Economy Process

Reinforcement Schedules

If you're reading this book, you are more than likely a teacher of sorts. Which means that you hear your name being called roughly 487,453,981 times an hour. Ok, perhaps that's an exaggeration but the point is that your students are often saying your name. They need help…they need directions repeated…they need a bathroom break. A fun little tool to address this constant repetition of your name is to use a visual reinforcement schedule. To do so, use something like different colored pieces of paper or leis, to indicate the availability of reinforcement. For instance, you may wear a green lei in your classroom during silent reading when it is ok for your students to approach your desk to talk and you may wear a red lei when they are not allowed to approach your desk. Or you may flip a card at the front of the room or put a cone on your desk—you get the point here. This tool can be used for more than just saying your name! Some other ideas for using this are below.

Letting your students know:
- When the bathroom breaks are allowed.
- When sensory breaks are allowed.
- When they can get up to sharpen their pencils.
- When alternative seating is available.
- When their devices can be used.
- When they can get help from their classmates.

SHOW ME!

NOTES:

Chapter 8:

The Drive

Motivation

Have you ever observed a student and thought, "Why are you doing that?" A motivating operation (MO) is what drives us to engage in certain behaviors. Let's discuss.

MOs alter behavior by changing the value of the reinforcers. Let's say you haven't had anything to eat today. Not eating makes food more valuable to you and increases the likelihood that you will go through the drive-through, make a trip to the grocery store, or cook dinner. On the other hand, if you have just eaten lunch, food is less valuable to you right now, so you are less likely to engage in those behaviors. The same is true for your students!

If your student has access to their iPad during free time and then you try to use it as reinforcement for completing a work task independently, they may be less motivated to complete the work than if they hadn't been on it for an extended time.

If your student has already earned two homework passes and then you try to give homework passes as the prize for winning vocabulary bingo, they may be less motivated to participate than they would if they didn't have two already.

Moral of the story? You want your students to be motivated, so you may need to manipulate things a bit to make that happen. Consider reinforcement satiation and deprivation when determining what reinforcers to use.

Superhero Secret:
If your student has free access to a reinforcer, they will be less likely to work for it. Limit access to items that you want to use to motivate them to work.

NOTES:

Chapter 9:

It's Not a Bad Word

Consequences

Many people think that consequences are always negative. By definition, consequences are whatever occur *after* the behavior, whether it's positive or negative.

By manipulating the consequences, we can cause behaviors to increase or decrease in the future. Cool, huh?

There are four things we need to remember when delivering consequences.

1. Consequences are contingent on the behavior. The reinforcer you are offering is ONLY available when the student engages in the target behavior(s).

Chloe can get the marshmallow if she stays in her seat but NOT if she is out of her seat.

2. Provide consequences immediately following the behavior. You must deliver the reinforcers IMMEDIATELY after the correct behavior has occurred (we

are talking seconds here). The more time that goes by, the larger the chance of another behavior happening, and you inadvertently reinforce *that* behavior.

Chloe gets a "Great job!" within three seconds of answering a question correctly.

3. <u>Appropriately size all consequences</u>. You don't want to provide too much or too little of the reinforcer for the effort provided.

If Chloe is matching words to pictures and you provide her a large bag of her favorite chips for a correct match, she may not be motivated to do any more matching—as she is burned out on what she was working for already. On the other hand, if she completes a 150-problem math test, one chip won't suffice.

4. <u>Consider the student's motivation</u>. A reinforcer will only work if it is available during specific times. When working toward a skill, be sure to withhold the item for a period of time so the student really wants it!

If Chloe just had ice cream, chances are she may not be as interested in completing a task that will be rewarded with ice cream.

Whether you know it or not, you are using consequences!

Positive Reinforcement

Positive reinforcement is the most widely used strategy in applied behavior analysis. Why is that? It's the most effective strategy with the fewest adverse side effects. Positive reinforcement adds something to a situation to cause an increase in the behavior. It sounds more complicated than it is. An example of this may include giving your student a high five for a correct answer. If they answer more questions correctly next time—you have used positive reinforcement! If they don't, you have not. This means you won't know if you are using positive reinforcement until AFTER you see if the behavior changes (or not).

Superhero Secret:
When using social praise as a reinforcer, be sure you are varying what you say. Don't "good job" them to death! Instead try "I love how you're sitting," "Beautiful handwriting!," "You are a rockstar!"

There are two main types of reinforcers: primary and secondary.

Primary reinforcers are those we are born inherently "knowing." No one needs to teach us to want them. These are reinforcers that everyone needs, and when you don't get them, you will seek them out. Examples include food when you are hungry, a drink when you are thirsty, or sleep when you are tired.

Secondary reinforcers are those that are provided along with primary reinforcers until they become their *own* reinforcers. Remember when we talked about pairing? We use that here! This is best explained with an example:

You are teaching your student to clap her hands. When they successfully do so, you give them their favorite cracker and, AT THE SAME TIME, say, "great job!" By doing this, they will eventually clap just for the praise.
Primary reinforcer: cracker (food)
Secondary reinforcer: praise

The reason this is important is because sometimes it seems that students do not have many interests. Some students want to sit and flap their hands all day or only play on the iPad. We pair secondary reinforcers to teach them to become interested in other things and expand their repertoire of items/people/places/activities/things they enjoy.

Positive Reinforcement vs. NCR

Positive reinforcement is different from the non-contingent reinforcement (NCR) that was previously discussed in that the learner has to engage in a predetermined behavior to EARN the item/activity/etc. The reinforcer is contingent on the behavior occurring. With NCR, they receive the reinforcement for free!

There are five different types of positive reinforcers you can use in the classroom:

- Social: This includes praise or attention of any kind. It can be something subtle like a thumbs up or a smile, or it can be a vocal response like "Way to go! You are SO SMART!"
- Edible: This may include things to eat and drink. Examples will be specific to the individual but may include a pretzel, a blueberry, a piece of candy, or a small sip of a favorite drink.
- Activity: These are activities the student enjoys. Examples may include playing a favorite game, reading or listening to a story, coloring, or blowing bubbles.
- Tangible: These are items the student likes. It may include an iPad, a favorite toy, a homework pass, or a special item in the classroom that they must earn and they value!
- Sensory: These provide some kind of sensory feedback to the student. Examples may be tickles, flashing lights or pinwheels, and different sounds or smells.

Superhero Secret:
When using food as a reinforcer, you want to switch over to something else as quickly as possible. Using high sugar or fattening foods can be detrimental to the long-term health of the student.

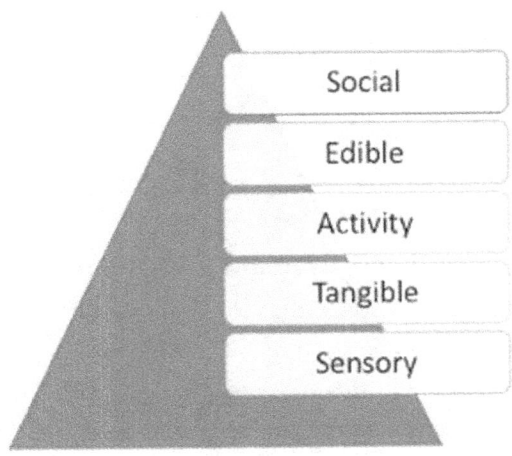

Types of Reinforcement: SEATS

As you can imagine, there are tons of items and activities that can become reinforcers. What is relevant here is the effect they have on the behavior. Does this item/attention/activity/sensory experience/tangible increase the preferred behaviors? If so, yep—it's a reinforcer! If not, keep looking.

Extinction

Superhero Secret:
Be sure you have tried other methods of behavior change before using extinction. If you do decide this is the best route, always use it in conjunction with teaching replacement behaviors.

Extinction occurs when a previously rewarded behavior no longer earns rewards, causing it to lessen or stop altogether. Many people assume that extinction means ignoring a behavior, but there is actually a lot more to it. You put a *behavior* on extinction, not a person. In order to put a behavior on extinction, one must first understand what the function of the behavior is.

If the function of the behavior is attention, the teacher would put the behavior on extinction by not providing attention. Let's say a student keeps falling out of his desk so that the teacher will reprimand them (give them attention). If the teacher stops reprimanding the student, soon their behavior will cease because it is no longer giving them the attention they are looking for.

Extinction Burst

When you use extinction, it is important to keep in mind that the behavior may actually increase before it decreases. This is called an extinction burst and is totally normal and to be expected. Stick with it and don't give up before the ABA magic happens (and the behavior decreases)!

Differential Reinforcement of Alternative Behavior (DRA)

We often use a procedure called differential reinforcement of alternative behavior (DRA) to reinforce preferred behaviors that are occurring in place of problem behaviors in an effort to increase those preferred behaviors. The problem with using extinction alone is that it doesn't teach any new behaviors. The student who no longer receives reinforcement (attention) by falling out of his desk may just discover another creative way to get you to pay attention to him.

DRA is two-fold. When using this method you will withhold reinforcement as you did with extinction, but ALSO teach an alternative behavior. Ultimately, we want the student to not have any desire to engage in the problem behavior. For example, when your student falls out of his seat, you will ignore that behavior and continue with the lesson. This is the "extinction" part of the procedure. For the other part, you will teach them how to get your attention in a more appropriate way (possibly raising their hand). Doing these two procedures together will decrease the problem behavior of falling out of his seat while also increasing his hand raising. DRA is an easy and successful way to decrease problem behaviors in the classroom.

Punishment

Punishment is used when we add something to a situation (such as a reprimand) or remove something (such as timeout from an activity or moving a card down on a behavior chart), and the behavior lessens. We use punishment as a last resort because of the negative effects it can have on behavior. These are things to consider when using punishment:

- The student may become more aggressive or become emotional.
- The student may get used to the punishment causing it to not be effective.
- The student may begin to avoid you/school/situations.
- The behavior may only go away temporarily.
- The behavior may decrease at school but increase at home.
- The student doesn't LEARN anything new or different when punishment is used.

I know what you are thinking: but we use this all the time! It's TRUE! Individuals who don't know its long-term effects use punishment all the time. Now that you do, let's agree this should only be used as a last resort, ok? This means that you will be sure to try many preventative strategies and reinforcement before using punishment.

On the rare occasion that a punishment procedure becomes necessary, apply it systematically. This is the procedure you will use before implementing a punishment procedure:

Take ABC data to establish function and frequency

Establish what reinforcement procedure to use

Select a punishment procedure

Superhero Secret:
Planned ignoring sounds a lot like extinction but is different in that
planned ignoring is only used when the function is attention.

Planned ignoring is a common punishment method used. It should be used ONLY when the data shows that the purpose of the behavior is to get attention (and is not dangerous). When this is the case, using planned ignoring can be an effective strategy to decrease the behavior. This is shown in the following example:

Steve, a tenth grader in your Spanish class, rolls his eyes. You have called him out on it, and it happens more often.

This means you have been inadvertently reinforcing the behavior. If the cause of the behavior was to get your attention and you withhold it, the behavior will decrease.

Using planned ignoring, you don't respond in any way. This means:
- Don't make direct eye contact.
- Keep neutral body language.
- Don't talk to or about Steve.
- Don't tell Steve you are ignoring him.

Another procedure that reduces problem behaviors is the use of a response-cost. With this method, the student loses something that was previously reinforcing for them. A common example of this is a classroom behavior chart where markers are moved up and down based on problem behavior.

Response blocking is used when you physically prevent the problem behavior from occurring. This may be done by utilizing a lockbox over the office call button in order to prevent a student from repeatedly pushing it or locking your desk so a student cannot take items without permission.

Superhero Secret:
If you have a particularly dangerous or self-injurious behavior, please
consult with a BCBA. They will be able to decide if a punishment
procedure is appropriate and assist in implementation.
Don't do it alone!

When we ask teachers how they address behavior in their classrooms, nine out of ten times they tell us "time-out" or "a behavior chart". Not only are these two tools overused, but they are often incorrectly implemented.

Time-Out

Time-out is a common practice in schools, especially in the younger grades. Bill pushed Sam at recess? Time-out! Leigh Anne told Shariece she was stupid? Time-out! Time-out, or removing an activity, item, or person in an effort to decrease a problem behavior, is a one-size-fits-all response to any behaviors that occur, regardless of the function. As we discussed more in-depth in the section on functions, if the behavior occurs because they want to escape the activity/person/place, then you are actually giving them exactly what they want!

In addition to using time-out to reinforce problem behaviors, we also see teachers use it as a replacement for teaching new skills. Bill pushed Sam at recess because he wanted a turn on the swing? Have we tried teaching Bill appropriate social skills to request taking a turn and reinforcing that? Leigh Anne told Shariece she was stupid because she wanted to make her other friends laugh? What about teaching her about the difference between kind and unkind actions toward friends and reinforcing the kind actions? Or what about teaching her some jokes?!

So let's say you've tried other non-punishment tools, like teaching new skills and reinforcing those skills and all of the other things you have learned about in this book. The behavior still occurs? Well, in that case, time-out may be a good option for you. The kicker is you need to implement it correctly. How do you ensure you're doing it correctly? Well, you're in luck! We've made you a list:

1. Determine the function so that you can make sure you aren't reinforcing escape-maintained behavior.
2. Stay calm—there is no room for cruelty, raised voices, or humiliation in a classroom setting.
3. When the behavior occurs, teach appropriate replacement behaviors.
4. When the behavior continues during time-out, do not allow the time-out to end.
5. Make sure the behavior is decreasing. If not, it's time to reevaluate.

Here are a couple of scenarios to think through:

Scenario 1: Ms. Jones is in the art room with her preschoolers during art class. Kia repeatedly knocks her paint over, as she does every morning. Ms. Jones has taken data and figured out that the function of this behavior is automatic/sensory.

Don't: Ms. Jones sends Kia over to sit by herself for the rest of art class at a different table.

Do: Ms. Jones takes Kia's paint away and calmly says, "You keep spilling your paint. We'll try again in a few minutes." A few minutes later, she sits with Kia and reintroduces the paint, providing praise and prompts for appropriate usage. Later, Ms. Jones may explore other replacement behaviors to address Kia's sensory needs. Kia has a time-out from her paint.

Scenario 2: The class is divided into two teams and Monica and Shelley are the team captains. When it is her team's turn, Monica screams the answers loudly. Her teacher, Mr. Chan, has taken data and determined the function is attention.

Don't: Mr. Chan yells "That's it, Monica, go into the hall!" in front of the class. While in the hall, several students stop by and chat with Monica.

Do: Mr. Chan calmly asks Donald to step in as team captain for a few turns before allowing Monica to step back in as captain. Monica has a time-out from being captain.

Scenario 3: Dr. Sidiqui's 3rd graders are completing a STEAM activity using dowels and marshmallows. Ben repeatedly hits his nearby classmates with his dowels. When reprimanded, Ben begins to yell and cuss at Dr. Sidiqui. Dr. Sidiqui has taken data and determined that the function of Ben's problem behaviors is usually attention.

Don't: Dr. Sidiqui yells, "Ben! I told you to stop! Go to the principal's office." In the principal's office, Ben gets to sit on the principal's couch and eat candy off his desk.

Do: Dr. Sidiqui calmly asks Ben to go sit in the pod outside of the classroom door. After Ben calms down, Dr. Sidiqui reminds him of appropriate behavior during the activity and allows him to rejoin the class. Ben has a time-out from the activity.

Behavior Charts

If you walk into an elementary school classroom, chances are high that you will see some form of a behavior chart. Horses running out of a barn, colorful cards, clips on a rainbow spectrum… you name it, we've seen it. Whatever the theme, the idea is mostly the same: a student is able to make progress toward a prize for preferred behaviors and they are punished (move your horse, flip your card, clip down) for problem behaviors. Cute, right?! Well, just like time-out, there are a few problems with these commonly used behavior charts. First off, we find that they actually are not that successful. When we asked those same teachers if their behavior charts or time-outs were effective in decreasing problem behaviors, we often find that they are not. Teachers rely solely on the chart and are not making any efforts to increase preferred behaviors or teach new replacement skills. Or what if the student's behavior is actually for attention? Calling their name, having them walk over and move their marker, and sending home a note to mom sounds like a whole lot of attention to us! If you are set on using one of these in your classroom, we recommend following guidelines that are similar to time-out procedures.

1. Determine the function so that you can make sure you aren't reinforcing attention-maintained behavior.
2. Stay calm—there is no room for cruelty, raised voices, or humiliation in a classroom setting.
3. When the behavior is not occurring, teach appropriate replacement behaviors.
4. Consider reinforcing more often. One student may be able to wait until Friday to choose something from the treasure chest, but other students may need daily or hourly (or more!) reinforcement.
5. Make sure the behavior is decreasing. If not, it's time to reevaluate.

<u>NOTES:</u>

Chapter 10:

The Toolbox

Teaching Technology

U p until now, we've spent a lot of time discussing how to address problem behaviors, but to do so, we must also teach our students new skills. This section describes specific teaching methods we use to teach appropriate behaviors and to decrease problem behaviors. You can use these technologies independently or in combination to meet the student's needs.

Errorless Teaching

Teacher: "Name an animal that lives in the ocean."
Student: "Water...boat...fish!"

D oes your student scroll through several possible answers when you ask them a question?
Do you have a student who just doesn't seem to be "getting it?"

Does your student repeatedly make the same mistakes over and over, even after you correct them?

Errorless teaching is an evidence-based practice in which we prevent the child from making a mistake. WHAT?! But making mistakes is an essential part of learning, right? Not always.

First, let's explore traditional teaching:

The teacher asks the student a question: "How old are you?" The student enthusiastically responds incorrectly or scrolls through some possible answers: "2, 200!" The teacher smiles because the child is adorable and trying so hard: "Good trying! You're 5!" The next time the teacher asks the student the same question, they giggle and shout "400!"

Now, what just happened here? We'll tell you: The teacher unknowingly reinforced the child's incorrect answer by smiling and giving praise which caused the behavior (guessing incorrectly) to occur again.

Let's look at another scenario in which we use errorless teaching.

The teacher asks: "How old are you?"
Before the student responds, the teacher immediately says, "Five."
The student repeats, "Five!"
The teacher immediately repeats the question or with holding up 5 fingers: "How old are you?" and prompts with just the f sound: "/f/."
The student says, "Five!"
The teacher praises the student for answering correctly.

Going forward, the teacher continues to back off the prompting and provide more reinforcement for more independence. Make sense? They prevent the student from making errors and reinforce the correct behavior.

We can also use errorless teaching when teaching communication skills.

For example, when teaching a child to communicate using sign language, we may start by showing the child something we know they really like, like a cookie. We would lay out a cookie and say "cookie" while modeling the sign "cookie." We would then immediately take the child's hands and help them to make the sign "cookie." Next, we would give them a small piece of cookie. We would continue this process while fading the prompts and providing larger pieces of a cookie for more independent responses.

Another way to use errorless teaching is as a strategy to avoid problem behaviors from occurring in the first place.

You have a student who holds on to your head to balance while you change his pull-up. They have occasionally pulled your hair. To prevent this from developing into a problem behavior, you hand-over-hand place their hands on the wall for balance. Over time you fade the prompt while reinforcing them when they put their hands on the wall until they independently grab the wall for balance.

In the examples above, you've probably picked up on two important parts to remember when implementing errorless teaching: reinforce and fade. Check out the steps below. We bet you'll be amazed at how quickly your students become independent using this strategy!

1. Gain the student's attention.
2. Present the question or instruction.
3. Immediately prompt the correct answer.
4. Conduct a "transfer trial" by representing the question or instruction and waiting 3 seconds to give your student an opportunity to respond independently.
5. If they respond independently, give a big reinforcer and move on to the next target.
6. If your student does not respond independently, represent the question or instruction and immediately prompt the answer. Give a very small reinforcer and move on to the next target.

Discrete Trial Teaching (DTT)

This teaching procedure is a structured way to teach a specific skill using reinforcement. It can occur when working with a student one-on-one at a table or more naturally throughout the school day. When preparing for DTT, helpful tools may include a datasheet, flashcards, manipulatives, known reinforcers, and a timer. The duration of the DTT trial and the number of trials per day will vary based on the child's developmental level, the staff's availability, and the school schedule. Common skills taught during discrete trial teaching may include:

- Identification of letters, numbers, shapes, etc.
- Labeling
- Imitation skills
- Repeating sounds, words, and phrases
- Personal information questions
- Matching skills
- Academics
- Fill-in-the-blank questions
- Fine motor skills

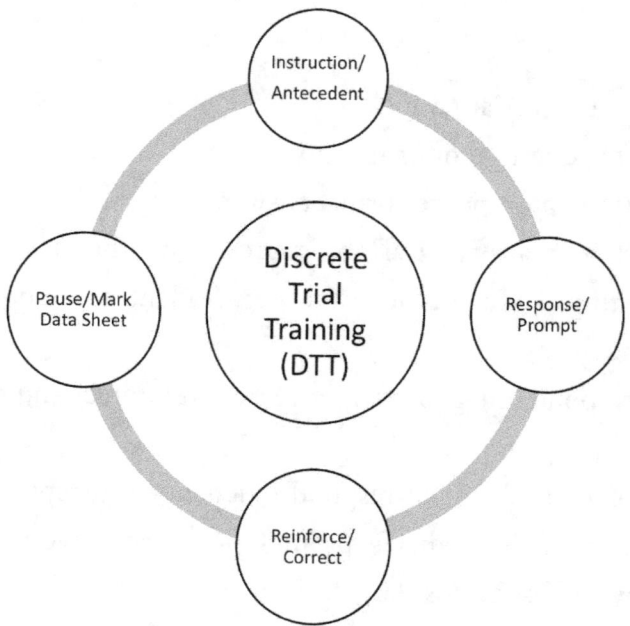

Natalie L. Perkel, Ph.D., BCBA & Beverly G. Smith, M.Ed., BCBA, LBA

The first DTT trial of each day will be known as the "cold probe." During this time, you will test the child to see what targets they have remembered from previous training and to see what skills you need to teach next. You only take data based on this one trial for the day. For all additional trials, you will use errorless teaching.

Once a target skill is correct three days in a row, put it aside and do not work on it for seven days. One week later, check to see if the student is still able to correctly respond (do another cold probe). If so, the skill is mastered! You'll want to periodically check all mastered skills to ensure the student retains the information.

Cold Probe Process:

1. Gain the student's attention. Say, "first we are going to work, and then you will get a cookie (or whatever reinforcer you are using)". Be upbeat, energetic.
2. Present the question or instruction. For example, "what is this?" while holding up a card showing the letter A. This is the cold probe.
3. Wait three seconds.
4. If the student answers correctly, give praise and a big reinforcer (whole cookie) and mark your data sheet with +.
5. If the student doesn't respond or responds incorrectly, give them a mastered target and move on to the next target.

If the student doesn't respond or responds incorrectly again, repeat the prompting procedure above once more before moving to the next target. Feel free to switch up the types of prompts you use.

Teaching Trials Process:

For every trial after the cold probe, you will use errorless teaching. You won't take data on these trials. The procedure is the same as above, except you do not wait three seconds for the child to independently respond; you immediately (within one second) prompt the correct response.

Errorless Teaching Process:

1. Gain the student's attention. Say, "First we are going to work, and then you will get a cookie (or whatever reinforcer you are using)." Be upbeat, energetic.

2. Present the question or instruction. For example, "what is this?" while holding up a card showing the letter A. This is the cold probe.

3. IMMEDIATELY prompt the correct answer. (What letter is this? A.)

4. Conduct a "transfer trial" by representing the question or instruction and waiting 3 seconds to give your student an opportunity to respond independently.

5. If your student responds independently, give a big reinforcer (whole cookie) and move on to the next target.

6. If your student does not respond independently, represent the question or instruction and immediately prompt the answer.

7. Give a very small reinforcer and move on to the next target.

One other option with the errorless teaching process is to use a distractor trial by giving the question or instruction for an easy, already mastered target before representing the new question or instruction.

Example of Motor Imitation using Errorless Teaching:
Teacher: Do this. (Claps hands). Immediately provides hand-over-hand prompting to clap the student's hands.
Teacher: Do this. (Claps hands).
Student: Claps hands.
Teacher: Great job (Gives small piece of candy).

Natural Environment Teaching (NET)

When teaching new skills, we want to make sure that our learners can generalize those skills into the real world. One way to ensure this is to practice those skills in the natural environment. NET can be done in the child's home, community, classroom, playground, lunchroom, etc. With NET, the child takes the lead, and you take advantage of their motivation to focus on areas of weakness. Address those deficits while the child is playing or engaged in their normal, everyday activities. This form of instruction is especially beneficial and easy to implement in classrooms.

Real-World Examples:

During centers, you see Ricky interested in the books. While he is looking at The Giving Tree, *you approach him and ask him a question about the main character or what is happening in the story. You provide prompts as needed to assist in answering the questions.*

While your class is on bathroom break, you notice SallyAnn standing too closely to Tryna in line. You prompt her to move by using a verbal reminder and modeling appropriate social distance from others.

Behavior Skills Training (BST)

When teaching a new skill, such as how to solve a multiplication problem, greet a new person, or zip your jacket, you can use BST to teach your student the new expectations and then show them what to do. There are four steps involved in BST:

1. Give directions by using clear and specific language to explain the expected behaviors to the student.
2. Model exactly what you want to see them do.
3. It's their turn! Rehearse by having them perform the task while you observe.
4. After observing them perform the skill, provide feedback by letting them know what they did correctly and how they can improve. As always, reinforce, reinforce, reinforce! (But remember to only reinforce the behavior you want to increase in the future).

Superhero Secret:
We can use BST with classroom staff, paraprofessionals, parents, and other related service providers. Use it during pre-planning to set expectations for your parapros before any problems arise.

Verbal Behavior

Many times, students will have problem behaviors because they don't have an effective communication system in place. Imagine if you were unable to express your wants and needs to others—you may become very creative in how you attempt to communicate.

- Tyrone can't open the milk carton, so he hits his teacher to get help.
- Rosie steals a pencil from a classmate because she is unable to ask if she can borrow it.
- Tia hits her head when she has a headache but is unable to tell anyone.
- Shawn runs from the table when he wants to take a break from work but is unable to ask for one.

The verbal behavior approach is how we teach communication skills. This approach is a bit different from traditional communication training in that it focuses on the function of language. It includes spoken and non-spoken language, such as sign language, Picture Exchange Communication System (PECS), assistive technology, and text. With the verbal behavior approach, you teach your students to ask for the items they want, label items, answer questions, imitate, and much more. In fact, there is so much involved in teaching verbal behavior that we cannot possibly cover it in this text—it is its own beast! Although this approach isn't well-known in the education world, it is extremely important and effective. We encourage you to check out the following resources to learn more about verbal behavior and how it can be beneficial in the classroom.

Verbal Behavior Resources

- **Verbal Behavior by B.F. Skinner**
- **The Verbal Behavior Approach by Mary Barbera**
- **Applied Behavior Analysis by Cooper, Heron and Heward**
- **Behavior Analysis for Lasting Change by Mayer, Sulzer-Azaroff, and Wallace**

Functional Communication Training (FCT)

FCT is, to put it mildly… AMAZING. It is a procedure that teaches communication skills, so individuals have no need to engage in problem behaviors. They can just *ask* for what they want. What?! This is especially significant for those students without a communication system in place, but even those who can ask for what they want sometimes need help in this area.

To start, when we talk about communication, we are talking about any kind of communication—vocal speech, sign language, Picture Exchange Communication System (PECS), alternative communication devices, etc. We group it all under the umbrella of verbal behavior. It's a little confusing for some as it seems that verbal = speaking, but that's not the case in ABA. Verbal behavior = all communication.

The first step is to figure out which system is best for the student. This is a community decision! Everyone involved in the student's academic/social/personal life should weigh in on this. If it is possible to get a speech evaluation, that would be helpful. Whatever the team decides, it should be used in all settings. Too often, students (usually early learners) will have some signs and some vocal speech. This can be really confusing for them. For example, if they know the answer to a question you ask, do they sign it? Say it? Use their communication device? As adults, we can recognize how difficult it is to learn a new language. Imagine learning three at once.

Superhero Secret:
NEVER take away a student's mode of communication. That would be like putting a piece of duct tape over their mouth. Students should always have access to their communication device, PECS, or other means of communication.

Sign Language Considerations

- Does the student have appropriate fine motor skills?
- Is the student able to imitate fine motor actions?
- Do you know sign language (or is there someone who can teach you and the student at school)?
- Is the family able and willing to use this as their main source of communication with the student?
- Will the student have access to a full vocabulary?
- Will others in the community be able to recognize the signs?

PECS Considerations

- Does the student have appropriate fine motor skills and hand strength?
- What will happen if there is not a picture for the desired item?
- Do you have the resources to create pictures?
- What will happen if a picture is lost or damaged?
- Is the student/family able and willing to carry the PECS book around with them everywhere they go? (This is a must with this system—as this book is their voice.)
- Will the child have access to a full vocabulary?

Communication Device Considerations

- Will everyone be able to use and understand the device?
- Will everyone be able to keep it charged? Is a backup device needed?
- Are teachers/families willing to have it travel with the student?
- Is the program/device affordable or will insurance cover it?
- How user-friendly is the program?
- Will the student have access to a full vocabulary?

Now that you have committed, let's talk more about how to apply the communication method.

Let's say you have taken your data and found that every time you ask Maurice to start his math assignment (a subject he finds difficult), he takes off his shoes and tosses them across the room. The data suggests the reason he is taking off his shoes is to escape the task. With functional communication training, you can prevent this behavior from occurring by teaching an alternate and appropriate behavior, like teaching him to ask for help.

Steps to Implementing FCT. A lot of this you have already learned!

Step 1: Identify the problem behavior—is the student kicking? Ignoring you? Refusing work?

Step 2: Collect ABC data on what is happening before and after the problem behavior occurs.

Step 3: Identify the function.

Step 4: Consider other behaviors that may have the same function. What can we replace this with that meets the same need?

Step 5: Practice the new behavior multiple times a day.

Step 6: Think about how we can generalize this to other settings and people.

Step 7: Use errorless teaching and shape the response. Basically, when teaching the new word, provide part of the word and reinforce! Slowly you will start to require more of the word in order to provide reinforcement.

Step 8: Be sure not to reinforce the original behavior. You have a new plan now! Instead, when the original behavior occurs, pause and prompt the new, socially appropriate communication.

Step 9: Fade the prompts.

Step 10: Take data to see if your intervention is working. If we do this right, they will find the new behavior (communicating) MORE reinforcing than the previous behavior in which they were engaging.

Does this seem intimidating? Yes! It's really not though. Once you identify and start working on a replacement, the rest can happen quite easily. It may take time to teach the new communication skill, but once the student realizes it's so much easier to just ask for what they want, you will find that the language will start to increase, and the problem behaviors will start to decrease. Everyone wins!

Active Student Responding (ASR)

ASR is a super easy tool to use with a whole group that promotes interaction and makes sure that your students are paying attention. There are three types: choral responding, guided notes, and response cards.

Choral Responding

In most classrooms, the teacher calls on individual students to answer questions when they raise their hands. Choral responding is a teaching method that works wonders in groups. It is an effective strategy to use with questions where the answers are short and the same. Within this technique, the teacher will provide a signal and students will respond in unison. Doesn't this sound fun?

Steps to using choral responding:

1. Establish and teach the signal (ex. "When I raise my hands, everyone will answer together at the same time.")
2. Ask the question ("What is four times four?")

3. Pause
4. Give the signal (Raise your hands)
5. Students respond ("Sixteen!")

Guided Notes

Guided notes are worksheets that a teacher prepares with missing information. As the teacher gives the lesson, the students follow along and fill out the worksheets. Guided notes encourage active participation and ensure that the information written is indeed the most important part.

Roygbiv is an acronym for _red_ , orange, yellow, _blue_ , _green_ indigo, _violet_ .
Combining yellow and _green_ will make blue.
Combining _red_ and yellow will make _orange_

Response Cards

Response cards are visuals that students write their responses on, and then hold them up in unison. It could be a small dry erase board or even a sheet of paper. The teacher asks a question, pauses, and allows everyone to answer and hold up their individual card. It allows the teacher to see everyone's responses at once without singling out one particular student. Similar to choral responding and guided notes, response cards require active student participation. When we have all these other fun techniques to try in the classroom, why don't we try something new?

Video Modeling

With so many ways to teach these days, video modeling is a fun variation of modeling that uses videos to record and play the lesson. It can be useful in teaching a wide variety of skills such as self-help, social skills, and daily living skills, including procedures and rules. You can tailor the video to target exactly what skill or behavior you are looking to increase or decrease. Another benefit of using this teaching method is that once the video is recorded and introduced, teacher's assistants or parents can also use video modeling to review/teach the skills with the student to encourage generalization. It is relatively easy to create and implement. Do you have an iPad? There you go! You are halfway there!

Skills needed for this teaching method:
- Attention (for at least a short time)
- Imitation (ability to do something that another person is doing)
- Motivation (even if it's not a super fun activity, you can make it so with your mad-creative skills)

Before you implement any intervention, you will have followed the steps discussed in the above chapters and identified the problem behavior or skill deficit, written a goal that is measurable and appropriate, and taken baseline data.

Superhero Secret:
You can easily find free resources for using video modeling with a quick Google search.

Steps for Implementation:
1. Plan your script. What will you be acting out? What exactly will you be saying and doing? Will you need a task analysis (more on this later)?

2. Keep it simple, focusing on one skill or procedure at a time.

3. Record! Model the appropriate behaviors for the student. You can talk through the steps as you do it or record your voice after the video is complete. The video should be short and directly to the point.

4. Decide how often and when the video needs to be shown. Implement it naturally into the student's schedule. For example, show a video of navigating the lunch line right before lunch and not first thing in the morning.

5. Watch the video with your student.

6. Have the student complete the skill or procedure.

7. If going through multiple steps (like in a task analysis), it may be beneficial to stop after each step so the student can practice each.

8. Take data to make sure the student is making progress.

9. Fade the video once the student has mastered the skill.

Because of the ease of this particular type of teaching method, you can make changes easily and quickly. You can delete and start over if necessary, if steps are missed, or skip mastered steps and focus on new steps.

A variation of video modeling is self-video modeling. It uses the same protocol as the first but has the student participating AS THE MODEL. How fun is that?! Let's say we are trying to teach Darren how to pack his backpack up at the end of the day. In the video, he will watch himself get his bag, go to the teacher's desk to get his communication book, go back to his desk, and put the communication book and notebook inside before zipping it up.

Group Contingencies

Most of the time, when we are looking to change behavior, we are focusing on the behavior of one student. In a classroom full of students, this can be time-consuming. Group contingencies are strategies that EVERYONE can participate in! With these, one or more students' behavior determines the consequences for the group.

It's important to know the difference between the various contingencies so you can select which is best for a specific situation. You need to know the skill sets of your students before implementing any of these (don't do this on the first day of school). Everyone needs to know how to do the task asked of them and be able to complete it in the time you are requesting. If some students struggle with fine motor skills or are still learning cursive, you will not want to do any kind of group contingency involving writing an essay in cursive in a short amount of time. We always want our students to succeed in group contingencies! These can be good for having students build one another up and cheer each other on.

There are three main types of group applications that are easy to use in any classroom:

1. Dependent Group Contingency: Either one member or a small number of participants are to complete the required task. If they are successful, EVERYONE WINS! If they are not, no one does. Because this is DEPENDENT on one person or a small group, be sure that the person or small group is able to complete the task.

Jack is totally capable of finishing the ten-question math assignment everyone has been given before the bell rings for recess. You choose to use a dependent group contingency and reinforce the whole class with ten extra minutes of recess when Jack is successful. Jack is able to stay on track and focus on the assignment as the class is encouraging and cheering him on. Jack finishes; the whole class wins!

2. Independent Group Contingency: The entire class is given a goal. Everyone who completes it earns their own reinforcement. Those who don't complete it, do not. This is best described as "you are on your own!"

You have a token system set up in the class where everyone earns tickets. You offer ten extra tickets for everyone who has their bag packed and ready to go five minutes before it's time to leave at the end of the day. Did everyone do it? Everyone who did wins ten tickets! Those who did not, do not.

3. Interdependent Group Contingency: Each individual in the group works toward the goal. If EVERY MEMBER meets the goal, the entire group earns reinforcement. If one student does not succeed, the entire group does NOT earn reinforcement. This is a good one to use when students participate in group work. They work together to reach a common goal and are all reinforced. This, like the dependent contingency, can allow for very supportive students to work together and help each other. If used incorrectly, it can cause frustration toward peers.

You assign your students to teams. They are to read a paragraph on turtles and answer questions about the content together. If everyone on the team participates, they each get to pick between a turtle keychain or a turtle sticker. If there is a member who does not participate, then no one on the team earns the turtle prizes.

Please use discretion when using this—we do not ever want to cause any emotional distress or frustration in the classroom.

Good behavior game (GBG) is a strategy that you can apply to groups—yay! The purpose of this game is to reinforce appropriate rule following in the classroom while you are teaching. To do this, you split the class into two groups and give points for inappropriate behaviors exhibited by any member of the group. Be sure to explain thoroughly which behaviors may get them a point. When the game is over, each team adds up their points and the team with the lowest number of points wins! If the teams tie, everyone wins the prize! The success behind GBG lies in the student's self-regulation and willingness to work together as a team. Whenever you feel like your class has gotten off track, you can use this strategy to get everybody's head back in the game!

Contingency Contracts

Doesn't that sound fancy? These can actually be really fun and easy to implement! They should be used with learners who are developmentally able to understand the concepts involved. These contracts are agreements between you and a student and target one specific goal: a skill or behavior that you would like to increase or decrease.

The main parts of the contract:

1. Who is the contract between?
2. What is the intended outcome?
3. What is the timeline?
4. What happens if they do/do not uphold the contract?

When implementing a contract, there are several things to keep in mind:

- BOTH parties must be on board! If the student doesn't care, this will not be successful. Having them participate in the creation of part of the contract may allow for more success.
- Having a place to track success on the contract itself can visually show progress and assist in keeping the student on pace. Also, everything is in one place—goal, reinforcer, data collection system, and all!
- Be sure that the contract is attainable! If Andy has never gone more than two days without missing at least one homework assignment, it would not be fair to ask that she turn everything in for the month. How do we know what is attainable? We look at baseline data.
- Be sure that it has all the necessary components but is easy to read. If it looks complicated, no one will want to do it!
- Be positive! Instead of writing "Bryan will finally arrive to class on time" or "Jeannie will not punch her neighbor at lunch," say what WILL happen (if possible) and put a positive spin on it. For example, Bryan will arrive at class by 8:15 each morning for three days in a row and Jeannie will keep her hands to herself during the thirty-five minute lunch period.

These can be individualized based on the student's age and developmental level. For early learners, you can use images or words only, and for more advanced learners, you can have them track their own progress. This can lead to your students learning self-management strategies.

Contract

Task	Reward
Who: _Sarah_	Who: _Ms. R. (teacher)_
What: _Will keep her hands to herself while in circle time._	What: _Will get a surprise from the toy jar_
When: _The whole week_	When: _At the end of the week_

How well: _During circle time, Sarah will sit on her square and will not touch any other students for the duration of circle time._

Signature: _____ Date: _____

Signature: _____ Date: _____

	Monday	Tuesday	Wednesday	Thursday	Friday	Saturday	Sunday
Date:							
Success? If not, who did she touch and how many times?							

Sample Contract

Replacement Behaviors

Sometimes we focus too much on the behavior we want to decrease and not so much on other behaviors that we want to increase. Many times, you'll find that as those necessary "replacement" behaviors increase, you'll see a natural decrease in the problem behaviors.

Let's say you have a student who engages in problem behaviors during math each day. You take baseline data and realize the behaviors occur when they are having difficulty understanding a math concept. You suspect they misbehave to escape having to do math. If you teach them appropriate ways to ask for help, they will no longer need to engage in problem behaviors.

Now, what if you have a non-verbal student who engages in aggressive behavior that occurs when they are hungry? If the student is taught to communicate when they are hungry, there is no longer a need for aggression.

Teaching new skills to our students can have a huge impact and should always be our focus. There are many types of new skills and behaviors that can be taught, including:

- Play and leisure skills
- Social skills
- Self-help/adaptive skills
- Organizational skills
- Academic skills
- Coping skills
- Communication skills

When deciding which skills to teach, there are a number of ways to determine which skills the child still needs to learn. First, you can look at the results of a recent assessment. Second, ask yourself the following questions:

1. What replacement skills can you teach to decrease problem behaviors?
2. What skills will increase independence?
3. Are there parts of certain skills that the student finds frustrating or refuses to do?
4. What skills would the student be motivated to learn?

Once you determine which skill to teach, you can begin breaking it down into manageable parts.

Shaping

Shaping occurs when you take a behavior and reinforce slight changes in how the behavior looks to get it closer and closer to the goal. Let's say you have a student who is independently performing a task, but it's just not up to par yet. It's not exactly the way you want them to be doing it. You can shape this behavior.

For example, you want your student to try a new food. You may start with them allowing the food on the table while you provide reinforcement. Then you may move to having it on their plate, touching it, smelling it, touching it to their lip, licking it, taking a small bite, etc. As the student masters each of those steps, you reinforce the behavior. You do not reinforce behaviors that are a step backward. You are shaping each step until you reach the final goal—eating the new food.

Another example: You are working on public speaking with your high-school students. Your goal for them is to appropriately introduce themselves to new people. Using shaping, you reinforce the steps (making eye contact, shaking hands, etc.) that move the student closer to the desired end result.

Shaping is one of those tools you can use with a variety of behaviors, including:
- Gross motor skills
- Fine motor skills
- Social skills
- Self-help skills
- Communication skills
- Feeding skills
- Play skills
- Academic skills

What behaviors are you currently teaching in your classroom that you could shape?

Chaining

Do you feel like you're constantly repeating the same directions to your students over and over?

"Put your homework folder in the basket."

"Make your lunch choice."

"Write your name on your paper."

It's exhausting, isn't it?!

What if we told you that you could do a little extra work now and save yourself from having to repeat those instructions constantly?

Interested?

Of course you are!

We're talking about chaining. There are many important skills that can actually be broken down into a sequence of several smaller, manageable parts. Those can then be systematically taught.

The final product is called a task analysis.

When planning to teach a skill, first, you should think about what steps your student will need to know how to complete. You will be teaching one step at a time. This process is known as chaining. Once your student has mastered one step, you will move on to the next, as if you are adding another link in a chain. This may be very different from how you usually teach, but it is important to remember that it may be challenging for some students to remember multiple steps at once. While it may seem like this will take longer to teach a new skill, the learner will be more successful in the long run.

When determining which step to teach first, watch to see the steps the student can complete independently and which need to be taught. There are different ways to do this with your students, including backward and forward chaining.

Backward chaining is especially helpful when a learner gets easily frustrated or is having difficulty with motivation. You would complete all of the steps except the last one. The learner would complete the last step only and then receive their reinforcer. This helps them to start off on a successful note as they are being rewarded quickly. After mastering that step, the learner would complete the last two steps, and so on.

Your kindergarten student needs to learn their mom's phone number. You prompt them with the first nine numbers and teach them the last one. You would say: 555-123-456_ and teach them to say 7 and reward them. Once they can consistently respond independently and correctly for a predetermined number of trials, you would back up and teach the last two numbers (555-123-45_ _).

Natalie L. Perkel, Ph.D., BCBA & Beverly G. Smith, M.Ed., BCBA, LBA

With forward chaining, you teach the first step of the sequence until the student has mastered it, and then you help them complete the remaining steps. Once they have mastered that first step (and been rewarded), the student will complete the first two steps independently before you assist with the rest of the steps. You continue this process until all steps are able to be completed independently.

Using the same example, your high school student knows only part of their mom's phone number. You would start with teaching the first number they don't know.

You say: What is your phone number?

They say: 555-12_ _

You say: 3

They repeat: 3

You say: What is your phone number?

They say: 555-123

Once they are able to respond correctly and independently for a predetermined number of trials, you would move forward and teach the next number.

A task analysis is great for countless activities and skills—from shoe tying to logging into a computer. They can include visuals, only words, or checklists. As always, be sure to use positive reinforcement.

Superhero Secret:
We often combine different strategies in order to maximize student success. You may use various teaching technologies together to develop new skills, increase preferred behaviors, and decrease problem behaviors. For example, you may use reinforcement along with punishment, DTT along with errorless teaching, and extinction along with FCT.

<u>NOTES:</u>

Natalie L. Perkel, Ph.D., BCBA & Beverly G. Smith, M.Ed., BCBA, LBA

Chapter 11:

School Stuff

ABCs of IEPs

I n the school system, everything centers around a student's Individual Education Plan (IEP). This is a legal document developed by the student's team, including the student themselves. IEPs can be time-consuming and overwhelming. Some end up taking on a "cookie-cutter" appearance, while others are so loaded down with irrelevant information, they are hard to navigate. As much as they can be a pain in the you-know-what, they are required and can be a useful and necessary document if you follow the rules and put in enough effort at the beginning. They can even make your life a little easier if done correctly (gasp!).

Superhero Secret:
When writing appropriate IEP goals, it is important to look at the
big picture to be sure you are focusing on behaviors that will have a

meaningful impact on the student's life. For example, you may have a goal for identifying 5 letters now that will one day aid the student in reading signs in the community.

At times, it is easy to get caught up in the curriculum-focused world of education, but as behaviorally minded educators, it is critical that you focus on behaviors that will make a social impact on the student's life.

When planning IEP goals, ask yourself questions like:

"What skills are most meaningful for my student?"

"How will teaching this skill allow my student to become more independent?"

"Will learning this skill help my student attain other skills?"

When writing IEP goals, you want them to be specific, measurable, and attainable. What do we mean by specific? Well, obviously, we want the goal to focus on that particular student. So no more "cookie-cutter" goals. Let's put some effort into this. The more specific you are here, the easier it will be to implement because you've already completed the planning step. You also want to make sure that the behaviors you are selecting are observable. You won't be able to measure "knowing" or "learning." Focus on action words in your goals—behaviors you can see and can collect data on.

Superhero Secret:
In the back of your mind, remember this is an INDIVIDUAL education plan. It is written specifically for your student to help them be more successful in the school setting and, hopefully, in life.

Goals also need to be measurable. Now that you know exactly what you want your student to do (or not do), how will you measure it? You'll need data to analyze and determine if your student is making adequate progress.

Finally, goals need to be attainable. You want to set your student up for success. If the goal is too far-fetched, your student won't be able to earn reinforcement. No reinforcement equals no increase or decrease in the behavior. You'll want to consider timelines here as well. Are you giving your student enough time to reach the chosen goal?

Collaborating

Who's in charge here? YOU ARE! It's so exciting! Your students will be looking to you to educate and mentor them. You will be pulled in so many directions. This is a tremendous responsibility—how are you going to juggle it all?

You need to know who your people are! Why is this important? Because you need to know who to go to when you have questions, concerns, or when you just need another opinion. There will be students who will challenge you, and you will be tested! There will be situations that arise that were not covered in your education and training. Everyone on your student's team is a valuable member and can provide different and important information based on their expertise. Establishing these relationships with others will help create a community and prevent you from feeling isolated when things get tough.

Some of the individuals who may be part of the student's team:
- Parents
- General education teachers
- Special education teachers
- Speech therapists
- Occupational therapists
- Physical therapists
- School psychologists/counselors
- Private behavior therapists

- School behavior specialists
- Teacher's aides
- School and district coordinators
- Administrators

What are some of the answers these individuals can provide? Here are a few:
- How long has the student been engaging in this behavior?
- Has there been anything you have tried in the past that has been successful at increasing/decreasing this behavior?
- Does this behavior happen under any specific circumstances?
- How often does it occur?
- How do you respond when it happens?
- Is there a place it happens more or a place it NEVER happens?
- Does the behavior occur in cycles?

Whether you hold a team meeting or communicate via email, collaboration is the way to go!

There is often a chain of command that you will need to learn for your specific school concerning who to contact in different situations. However it goes, be sure to find out BEFORE things get tough.

Training Paraprofessionals

Schedules and layout and visuals, oh my! By the first day of school, our minds are spinning with all of the five thousand things we have done to prepare for our students' arrival. There is so much on our plates that we sometimes forget one of the most important things to do to prepare for the school year—training our paraprofessionals. Parapros, teacher's assistants, aides…whatever we call them, they are vital to our classroom running smoothly, our students being successful, and let's be honest—our job being enjoyable! Below we've outlined a process for using ABA to ensure that these goals are met.

1. Pair with them: You know how it's important for your students to love you before they're willing to work for you? Well the same is true for your paras! Start out with connecting yourself with their favorite things. Bring in a Starbucks on Day 1… compliment their new haircut… smile… be nice. If they like you, they'll want to do their jobs and do them well.

2. State your expectations: We've talked to teachers before who were upset with their parapro's behaviors and after a couple of discussions, we realized that the teacher had never sat down with the para to express their expectations. We strongly recommend sitting down during pre-planning and breaking down the schedule. Tell your para exactly what you want them to do during each part of the day and each activity. We love to make a separate "para schedule" letting them know exactly where they need to be and which students they are responsible for at that time. Just like with our students, be sure to clearly define the behaviors you are looking for. We can't expect them to read our minds!

3. Teach procedure: After clearly stating your expectations, it's time to teach them! Wait a minute—you can't just tell them what you want them to do and they do it? Nope! Using behavior skills training, or BST, will ensure that they know exactly what to do. You've already explained the specific expectations to them so all that is left is to model it for them, then have them perform the task/skill/procedure, and then provide feedback. This can be a little tricky when working with adults—especially if you are younger than your parapro. So, show them *exactly* how you want them to respond to off-task behaviors during circle time and *exactly* how you want them to use backwards chaining during hand washing and *exactly* how you want them to implement visuals during reader's workshop. It is just like teaching our students those first day of school procedures and it does pay off in the long run. Once you've taught them, have them practice them in real-time while you give them feedback. Tell them what you saw that was spot-on and where you could see improvement.

4. Evaluate: Your school probably has an evaluation system that you complete at the end of each semester. Be sure to review this with them and provide specific feedback.

Time	Class	Teacher	Para 1	Para 2	Therapy
8:00	Arrival	Car Duty	Bus Duty	Classroom Duty	
8:30	Circle Time/ Toileting	Teach Circle Time	Model/ prompt at circle time	Take students individually to the bathroom	
9:00	Small Groups	Individual Instruction on IEP Goals	Fine Motor/ Sensory Group	Reading Group	
9:30	Story Time	Read Story	Language Arts Inclusion	Model/ prompt at circle time	
10:00	Small Groups	Individual Instruction on IEP Goals	Fine Motor/ Sensory Group	Reading Group	Speech Therapy- T/Th
10:30					OT- M/W
11:00	Lunch/ Toileting	Lunch/ Planning Period	Take students individually to the bathroom	Supervise Lunch	
11:30	Recess	Supervise Recess	Supervise Recess	Lunch Break	
12:00	Rest Time	Supervise nap/ rest	Lunch Break	Supervise nap/ rest time	
12:30	Small Groups	Individual Instruction on IEP Goals	Fine Motor/ Sensory Group	Reading Group	
1:00	Circle Time	Teach Circle Time	Model/ prompt at circle time	Model/ prompt at circle time	
1:30	Snack/ Toileting	Take students individually to the bathroom	Supervise snack	Math Inclusion	
2:00	Dismissal	Car Duty	Bus Duty	Bus Duty	

Sample Daily Schedule

Positive Behavioral Interventions and Supports (PBIS)

PBIS is often used in schools, and even if you haven't used it, you have probably heard of it. It is a collection of strategies and rules used to teach pro-social/appropriate behaviors, thereby decreasing problem behaviors. It incorporates data collection to measure progress and it divides students into three subsets:

Tier 1-affects everyone on campus (teachers, students, administration, etc.), and is set up to decrease behavioral concerns and, in turn, increase the time students have to learn.

Tier 2-affects a small percentage of students who need additional support. This step aims to prevent problem behaviors from increasing by offering specific interventions for students who may have social, academic or emotional deficits.

Tier 3-affects a very small percentage of students and assists in providing support for individual students who have not responded to tier 1 and tier 2 methods.

Some of the strategies that are used when implementing PBIS may include: prompting, organizing the classroom, using visuals, establishing schedules, verbal praise, utilizing reinforcement systems, modeling, implementing antecedent strategies... do you get where we are going here? If you are using PBIS in the classroom you are already using evidence-based ABA strategies to increase/decrease/teach new behaviors.

Programming for Generalization and Maintenance

When we begin planning an intervention for our students, we need to have the end goal in mind. Do we just want our students to be able to perform this one taught skill with us here in our classroom? Heck no! We want them to generalize what we teach them to other similar skills in different settings, with different people, and under different conditions. This isn't something our students automatically know how to do—this needs to be planned for and taught. Think about it this way: let's say you've taught Marco to state his teacher's names. When you're in the hallway and the principal asks Marco whose class he is in, he is unable to answer. This student has mastered this question with you, but he isn't generalizing that skill to a new person (the principal) and setting (the hallway).

Thinking about these from day one is extremely important. Here are a few tips to remember:

1. Reinforce the preferred behavior in a variety of settings. One way to do this would be to reward your student for raising their hand before speaking in the classroom *and* during a school-wide assembly.

2. Use naturally occurring reinforcers. This could be done by encouraging a student's friend to give them attention when they take turns on the swings at recess.

3. Make sure problem behaviors aren't reinforced in other settings. Share strategies with others so everyone is responding the same when behaviors occur.

In addition to planning for generalization, you also want to plan for the maintenance of skills *over time*. We often hear teachers say that one of their students mastered a skill but now has "regressed." This tells us that someone along the way didn't consider the maintenance of that skill. To prevent your students from "losing" skills, those skills need to be periodically reinforced in different places and contexts.

Have you ever had a recipe for a favorite cake or a mixed drink? You loved it so much you thought you would never forget it. But after not making it for a while, you forgot and now have to look up the recipe to help jog your memory. Without practicing a skill every now and then, we are less likely to remember the details.

<u>NOTES:</u>

Chapter 12:

That's All, Folks!

Connecting the Dots

So, where do you begin? First, you will identify the problem behavior and collect baseline data. You will use that data to figure out why the behaviors are happening and consider replacement behaviors that can be taught. From there, you will teach those new behaviors and plan for generalization. Next comes the fun part! Here you will use the strategies you just learned to decrease problem behaviors, while reinforcing preferred behaviors and shaping the new response. Once the problem behaviors have decreased and the replacement behaviors are established, you will fade your prompts. Finally, you will take data to determine if your interventions were effective.

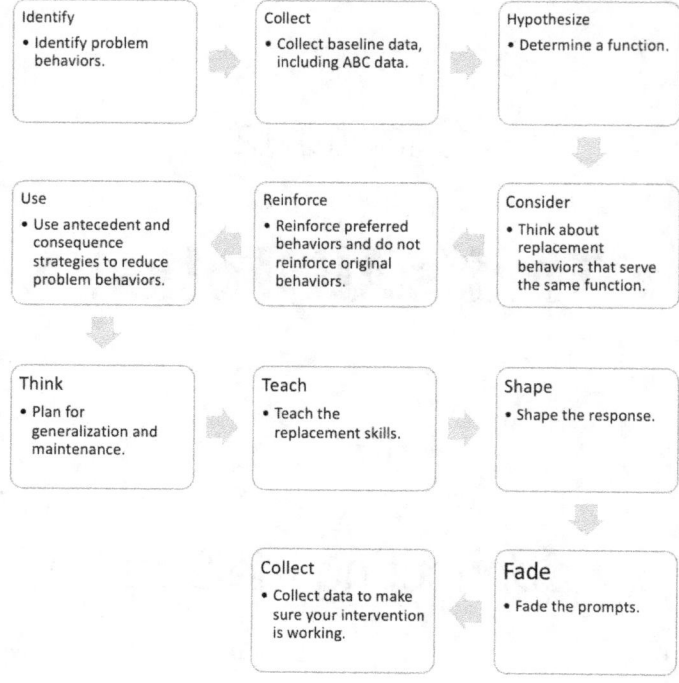

The ABA Process

All teachers want to have a classroom that runs smoothly. We want zero negative behaviors and 100% class participation. Below is a general list of tips for the classroom that may help keep things running smoothly.

Superhero Secrets

Don't talk about a student in front of that student (or in front of other students). Honestly, no one likes this unless you are saying good things about a person.

More language from you does not equal more understanding from students. Sometimes you will need to explain a concept further, other

Natalie L. Perkel, Ph.D., BCBA & Beverly G. Smith, M.Ed., BCBA, LBA

times you will need to explain it in another way (as in with visuals). Either way, keep things short and sweet.

Always follow through. Do what you say you are going to do—and that goes for reinforcers, consequences, and demands placed.

Shift your mindset. You don't just want them to follow your directions "because you said so," you want them to WANT to follow your directions.

Remember, change creates change. If what you are doing isn't working, you need to change what YOU'RE doing in order to change what they're doing.

All behavior is communication. Always go back to the function.

Lose the sarcasm. It's not nice. It's not helpful.

Don't lose your cool. Kids pick up on our energy. Stay calm.

Model positive language for your colleagues—if the lunch lady says "Wow, your class is so wild!" respond with "We sure have a lot of energy!"

Focus on the behaviors you want to see more of instead of the ones you don't. Try to praise five behaviors for every one that you correct.

The End

We don't know the exact situation that brought you to this book. Perhaps you are a new teacher and don't feel that your university education adequately prepared you to address the wide variety of behavioral needs in your classroom. Maybe you've been teaching for twenty years and you are fed up with trying the same things over and over with no results. You could be an administrator who has been out of the classroom for many years but you're hoping to help your teachers implement behavior strategies that really work. Whatever brought you to this point, we are glad you joined us on this journey. We hope that you found this material to be helpful in addressing behaviors in your classroom.

So how are you feeling? It would be so much easier to go back to what you have been doing and hope for change. But if you've made it this far we know that you are truly looking for a way to help your students.

Now it's time for you to don your superhero cape! Go back and review the information as needed and find us on Facebook (Behavior Queens) where we share helpful tips and resources. We encourage you to only make a couple of changes at a time and stick with it. We are confident you will begin to see positive changes in your classroom!

Natalie L. Perkel, Ph.D., BCBA & Beverly G. Smith, M.Ed., BCBA, LBA

THAT'S ALL, FOLKS!

<u>NOTES:</u>

References

Bailey, J. & Burch, M. (2016). *Ethics for behavior analysts* (3rd ed). New York: Routledge.

Bearss, K. et al. (2018). *Parent training for disruptive behavior: The RUBI autism network.* New York, NY: Oxford University Press

Cooper. J.O., Heron, T.E., & Heward, W.L. (2007). *Applied behavior analysis (2nd ed.).* Upper Saddle River, NJ.: Pearson/Merrill-Prentice Hall.

Franzone, E. (2009). *Steps for implementation: Functional communication training.* Madison, WI: The National Professional Development Center on Autism Spectrum Disorders, Waisman Center, University of Wisconsin.

Hetzler, Lynn. *7 Myths about applied behavior analysis.* Relias, 1 Sept. 2020, https://www.relias.com/blog/myths-about-applied-behavior-analysis.

Mayer, G., Azaroff, B., & Wallace, M. (2014). *Behavior analysis for lasting change* (3rd ed.). Cornwall-on- Hudson, NY: Sloan Pub.

Page, LeAnne (2015). *Parent with science: Behavior analysis saves mom's sanity* BCBAToday.

Schramm, R., & Miller, M. (2014). *The 7 steps to earning instructional control: A program guide for developing learner cooperation with aba and verbal behavior.* Buckeberg: Pro-ABA.

Dear Behavior Queens,

I'm a first-year teacher and I'm really struggling with one particular little girl in my class this year. She has Dandy-Walker Syndrome and uses a wheelchair. She doesn't speak and is legally blind. She cries almost all day long and bites the backs of her hands so badly that they are bleeding and scabby. I've tried everything with her to help her calm down! She really loves music and that seems to help, so I play it and hug her when she gets really upset but I'm not sure if that's working. Please help!

Sincerely,
Frazzled First-Grade Teacher

Dear Frazzled First-Year Teacher,

First things first—take a deep breath. It's obvious that you care a lot about your students and want to help them! With self-injurious behaviors like this, we always like to suggest that you reach out to a local BCBA to get specific directions. In order to choose the right intervention for your student, you'll want to first figure out why the behavior is happening (what's the function?). Is she biting her hands because it feels good...because she likes the attention you give her afterwards...because she gets out of work...maybe because she gets to listen to her favorite song afterwards? After you determine the function, you'll be able to choose an appropriate intervention. You'll also want to look at teaching replacement behaviors. For example, if the biting behavior happens because she likes the feeling of biting on something, perhaps she would like to bite on a chewy just as much. Knowing the function will help you here as well. Finally, be sure to take your data so you can make sure that your intervention is working! You can do this!

Sincerely,
Behavior Queens

Dear Behavior Queens,

I'm a 9th grade history teacher. I have this student who is extremely smart, well-spoken, and funny. The problem is, he's always speaking out of turn, making sarcastic jokes, and getting his classmates riled up. I try to stay calm and ask him to please wait his turn, calm down, etc. but there have been times where I get so frustrated, lose my cool, and raise my voice. The thing is, none of those things seem to be working. If anything, he seems to do it more! Would love to hear any ideas you have.

Thanks,
Helpless in History Class

Dear Helpless in History Class,

We love your honesty! As much as we try, we are all human and do sometimes get frustrated with our students. Having a set plan in place beforehand can help so much with this. The first thing we would recommend doing is figuring out why your student's problem behaviors are happening in the first place. This is so important because we could be accidentally reinforcing their behavior with our strategies. For example, if the function of his behavior is attention, your reprimands could be a reward to him and cause the behavior to happen more. Once you determine the function, you'll be able to implement an appropriate strategy and take data to make sure that the strategy is working. Good luck!

Best,
Behavior Queens

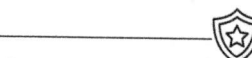

Dear Behavior Queens,

I teach a preschool class for students with special needs. I love working with these kids but I feel so lost! They are all so different- some are toilet trained and some aren't... some can talk and others can't... some can sit and follow directions and others run around the room constantly. I don't know where to start with them... what should I teach them first?!

Thank you,
Puzzled in Preschool

Dear Puzzled in Preschool,

Kudos for reaching out to us! Sometimes it's hard to admit that we are struggling or don't know what we're doing and it's so important to reach out to experts for help. We would strongly suggest completing an initial assessment with each of your kiddos—including parent interviews, observation, and a curricular assessment to let you know exactly what skills they have and what they still need to learn. From there, you may want to just focus on one or two skills per area, for instance you may choose one manding (requesting) goal, two tacting (labeling) goals, etc. If multiple students have the same goal, that will make your life easier because you can teach them at the same time! The VB-MAPP is a great curricular assessment to use and can help you map out a plan for what to teach next.

Sincerely,
Behavior Queens

Dear Behavior Queens,

I need your help with one of my third-grade students. She is doing pretty well but during silent reading every day, it's like she's a completely different kid! She cries, talks back, and refuses to read. Then as soon as reading is over, she's back to normal. It's the strangest thing! I tried to start a star chart with her and give her a star at the end of the week if she has good behavior every day during silent reading but that didn't help at all. Any suggestion on how to get her to behave would be great!

Sincerely,
Tired Teacher

Dear Tired Teacher,

We love that you're trying to find solutions for your student so that she enjoys this time more and doesn't engage in those troubling behaviors! Whenever our students are having specific difficulties with activities like this, it always makes us think about two things: response effort and reinforcement. Response effort is how hard the students has to work. The response effort for silent reading may be too high for this kiddo. You may want to look at shortening the amount of time that they need to read. Take some baseline data—if their behavior starts after five minutes of reading, you may want to start there and build up. Of course, you'll need to reinforce the behavior but only rewarding with one star per week may not be enough. Does the student even like the star sticker? You can complete a preference assessment and figure out what she realllllly likes and then use that! Start out reinforcing small intervals—like that five minutes we talked about before, and then slowly build up. Good luck!

Sincerely,
Behavior Queens

Dear Behavior Queens,

I feel like I shouldn't need to reach out for help because I am a veteran teacher of twenty-five years but I have a new student who has me stumped! I use discrete trial teaching for all of my students' individual academic goals (which I love!). I have this one student who swipes all of the materials off of the table.

Every. Single. Time. I'm at my wit's end here. I've tried pushing the materials over to my side, priming him before the transition to the table, and giving him a small piece of candy for every thirty seconds that he doesn't swipe. The candy worked for a minute but then it started again. I would love some new ideas for how this tired, old teacher can address this super irritating behavior.

Best,
Old Dog Needs New Tricks

Dear Old Dog Needs New Tricks,

Don't feel bad—we all are constantly growing and learning as our field changes and we come in contact with new kids and new behaviors. With your student, we would recommend first starting with taking some ABC data and determining the function of the behavior. This is so important! Let's say the function is escape. Maybe you aren't getting him up from the table or removing the work but if you're taking a few minutes each time to re-gather all of the materials, that is still escape and would still be reinforcing his behavior. Make sense? We would also suggest making sure the student is paired with the table/ DTT. Perhaps bring him to the table sometimes just to play with his favorite toy instead of work. Finally, make sure you are using effective reinforcers that are being delivered in an appropriate amount and at an appropriate time. It may not be enough reinforcement or it may not be presented quickly enough. Or it may not even be something he wants to work for. Hopefully these suggestions will help!

Sincerely,
Behavior Queens

Dear Behavior Queens,

I am a first-year teacher in a special education classroom. I have seven students and I love what I do but I feel like I have a lot to learn. My students are especially struggling with transitioning between activities. I feel like I'm seeing a lot of problem behaviors during those times. I know that I should be using visuals to help them but I feel lost. What visuals should I start with?

Thanks,
One Lost Teacher

Dear One Lost Teacher,

There are so many options and no perfect answer! If we had to pick which to begin your visual classroom, we would say start with schedules based on the developmental level of your learners. You may be able to make a class schedule or you may need individual schedules. Be sure to have one in place, even if you think your students don't need it/want it. It provides direction, predictability and supports what you say!

Sincerely,
Behavior Queens

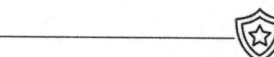

Dear Behavior Queens,

I need help! I am a new teacher who went through a non-traditional certification program so my background is not education, it is Biology. I've been placed in a high-school resource classroom and have about ten students who come to me throughout the day for extra academic help. They are a great group of kids but I find that I'm struggling with how to address behaviors that I am seeing. How do I decide which intervention to use?

Thank you,
New to This

Dear New to This,

There isn't really one right intervention. Actually, it may be that there are several different ones that could all be successful. According to the part of the seven dimensions that covers parsimony, we always want to start with the simplest techniques and then expand on them if needed. Remember: You will always begin by using positive reinforcement. You may start with using a simple reinforcement schedule where you give five extra minutes of free time for those who submitted work on time for a week. You keep a running tab of names that earned the extra time on the chalkboard. You could also use a token system to do this, where students keep track themselves. You could also use a behavior contract to show the exact same thing! None of these are the right answer, you will just have to experiment to see what works best!

Sincerely,
Behavior Queens

Dear Behavior Queens,

I teach middle school gen ed with mostly neurotypical kids and a handful of students with special needs, including learning disabilities and emotional-behavioral disorders. I have a very large class and few supporting staff this year and honestly just don't have time for data collection.

Sincerely,
What do I do?

Dear What do I do,

We totally hear you. Classrooms are busy places and data collection takes time and resources. However, when looking to change the behavior of others, it is crazy important that we know what the current rate of the behavior is. Is there any way you can borrow staff from another classroom for a short time? Can you recruit anyone in administration who can help? You will not need this help every day, only to establish a baseline and measure progress. If all goes well, that behavior will increase (or decrease) and you won't need the help for long! Also, be sure to check out our list of tips for data collectors!

Sincerely,
Behavior Queens

Dear Behavior Queens,

I am a high school teacher in a self-contained classroom. One of my students is a senior this year and has started engaging in a behavior he hasn't done before. He has been grabbing or pulling on his classmates. I tried taking ABC data and there is not an antecedent—it happens out of the blue. I think it's just that he wants to control everyone.

Sincerely,
Clueless in the classroom

Dear Clueless in the classroom,

We love that you tried taking ABC data - that's a great start! However, we would like to challenge you to look a bit closer at the antecedent. We know it seems like sometimes behaviors may happen "out of the blue," but there is always an antecedent. Maybe you were talking to another student or they were completing a math worksheet or the principal had recently poked their head in the classroom. It is super important that you figure out what that is because that is going to help lead you to the function of the behavior. If you recall, there are four functions of behaviors - attention, escape, sensory and tangible. It may seem like he wants to control everyone by physically moving them, but it could be that he is trying to get their attention or that he is trying to access some sensory input by grabbing/pulling on them.

Sincerely,
Behavior Queens

Dear Behavior Queens,

    I have a student who is constantly running out of my classroom. I've taken ABC data and figured out that the function is for attention. When she's wandering the halls, other school teachers and staff intervene and try to "help" by talking to her, trying to bribe her back to our room, etc. When this happens, her elopement behavior is always more for a few days after. How can I get everyone on the same page as far as not reinforcing her behavior with attention?

Thanks,
I don't need their "help!"

Dear I don't need their "help!,"

    Oh, that's one we see a lot in schools! We strongly recommend using some prevention strategies with your co-workers. Remember, ABA isn't just for our students! We recommend first starting with sending out an email or letter to everyone. Let them know what the situation is and give them ideas for how they can truly be helpful. Secondly, you may want to have a visual letting them know when they CAN interact with your student. (After all, you want to reinforce their preferred behaviors!) One idea is to wear a lanyard with a red and green piece of paper that you can turn to indicate when they can talk to your student and when they can't. That way they are still able to "help" but can do so without accidentally reinforcing problem behaviors.

Sincerely,
Behavior Queens